SPIRITUAL RESOURCES ARE AVAILABLE TODAY

VOLUME ONE

SPIRITUAL RESOURCES ARE AVAILABLE TODAY

An Exploration in the Ministering of the Holy Spirit

VOLUME ONE

BY

ROY A. CHEVILLE

HERALD PUBLISHING HOUSE

Library of Congress Catalog Card No. 74-21216
ISBN 0-8309-0138-8

Printed in the United States of America

CONTENTS

FORELOOK
INTO OUR
EXPLORATION

Explorers set out to discover more about some field of interest and of worth. They move out with intention to discover more as the journey proceeds. Ours is to be a continuing adventure.

The undergirding affirmation of our exploration is this: In this universe of ours are spiritual, God-provided resources for enabling man to achieve personhood of merit. The first statement of the title was, "Spiritual Resources for Developing Personhood." Basic is the assumption that these resources are available today as we understand and qualify for contact. This means that we harmonize with the purposes and processes of the Provider of these resources. Here these resources are identified as *Holy Spirit.*

This exploration proceeds with the view that during the centuries this ministering of the Holy Spirit has been neglected (which applies both to the experiencing of the Resource and to the interpreting of the Spirit). This brings to the fore a contemporary sense of urgency.

Darkness Where There Is Available Light

So often we humans live in the midst of resources and are unaware of them. We may ridicule the idea that resources even exist. Primitive men did this for centuries. They would squat in their cold, dark winter settings, unaware that beneath them and around them were resources of coal for heat and waterfalls for electrical power. If some wise newcomer had told them of these available resources, they might have scoffed at the idea. Such resources would have been consigned to the world of fancy and make-believe. So primitive men built their little fires for warmth and light. They kept to their own patterns and stayed with their own world of resources.

Today millions sit or shuffle or stride in relative spiritual darkness, unaware of spiritual resources in the universe. Much of the theology they have heard and much of the practice in their religious circles have tended to close out such resources as existent, as available, as practical. If some person were to come along and speak with clarity and with conviction about "available spiritual resources," the response might be that this person had never "thought through" what he was talking about. Or he might be dismissed as someone of weird imagination or impulsive expression. His talking would make for fancies and dreams, not for genuine happenings. A modern skeptic might be inclined to label it "spiritual fiction" when told of "available spiritual resources."

Inadequate Experimentation

Moderns might be inclined to try out what is recommended. They might try some quickie that would get returns in a hurry without requiring much, if anything, in discipline or understanding. Let there be a seance, a drug application, a physical posture for an all-at-once incoming of power. The why and the how would be replaced by the wham and the whoopie. It is fairly common in religion for people to want some return, some assurance all at once. A five-minute indulgence is more appealing than a ten-year program of living.

Worthful exploration calls for a longer, more purposive experimentation. In the field of spiritual resources this experimentation requires worthy insight, personal fitness, and laboratory experience in the business of living. This would be true in the field of physical resources for producing light and heat in the world of primitive man. It would call for more than wishing or working out some manipulating exercises for quick returns. The same applies to spiritual resources, which also call for maturing insight, worthy motivation, and sound laboratory living. It involves establishing right relations with the inclusive world of these resources and understanding that personhood of high quality comes to pass through longtime exercise and consistent operation.

When we explore we do not start out with all the answers and solutions. We do not even have all the questions. But we have a field in which we are certain that there is something for us to find out about, something that matters. It was so with geographical explorers who crossed oceans and mountains and plains to discover what was out there in the yet-unknown. They began with a working idea; they adjusted their pictures of things as they proceeded on their way. Some of their conceptions, some of their charts needed change. For instance, Christopher Columbus kept to the idea that the America he discovered was India. Often the land and the people were different from the descriptions of them carried back to Europe.

The real explorer keeps going. He keeps trying to find out more. He keeps changing conceptions as he goes on.

Spiritual Explorers Needed Today

This kind of outlook is needed in today's spiritual explorings. We need to hear the call of Kipling's Explorer: "Something out there. Go and find it." This calls for those who will proceed with open eyes and learn on the way. It requires dynamic, discipline, devotion. The explorer has to learn how to make contact with these spiritual forces, how to line up for this contact. He has to see what the Source of these spiritual resources has in mind, in purpose, in process. He needs to perceive what quality of person God has in mind for using them. The exploration is lifelong, eternity-long.

The need for this exploration is now.

Roy A. Cheville

SECTION A

Overviews
For Our
Exploration

This section comes first for orientation and foundation. It pictures the general setting in which our exploration proceeds. It involves the conceptual world in which the Holy Spirit is interpreted today. What we say has to be meaningful. Our portrayal is in the field of happenings that we call *personal,* and this is imaged in the light of our total universe. Basic are these postulates: (1) that there is spiritual reality in the universe; (2) that the functioning of these realities is *natural* and describable; (3) that the fullness of personal development requires contact with and utilization of these divinely provided spiritual resources in accordance with God's purpose and process. We use the term of our own Christian faith, the *Holy Spirit.*

A Call

For

Exploration

This field of considering the Holy Spirit has been fairly closed for a long while. Sometimes it was left alone, for leaders felt safer avoiding it. Sometimes it was assigned to the not-to-be-considered, because there was so little material of good quality about it. Sometimes it was as one commentator observed: "When something has been buried so long, there has to be a pretty good reason for digging it up." The time is ripe for exploration.

As Seen by Contemporaries

Recently a young man of a conventional church was asked, "Have you received the Holy Spirit?" He honestly replied, "I don't know what it is, so how would I know if I had ever had it?" This sounds like what happened in ancient Ephesus when Paul came there. He met disciples who had never heard of the Holy Spirit. Many a modern would be as confused as were those men of Ephesus.

A woman of intense pentecostal feeling testified how she had "got the Spirit" while she was standing in a bathtub, how she slipped, fell over and broke her arm. One listener said, "If that is where and how you get the Spirit, I don't want any of it." And then as an aside he asked a friend, "Just what is this Spirit she talks about?" A sophisticated churchman commented recently, "This Spirit stuff is out of date. Only fanatics would want it." And a hearer replied, "Then those early Christians must have been a bunch of fanatics." A youth in a Jesus group reported to a friend, "Did we ever have the Spirit last night!" When a friend asked about it, the one who had been in the Spirit-possessing meeting replied, "I can't tell you about it. You'll have to get it yourself if you are ever going to know." He was saying that the manifestations of the Spirit are not to be examined; they are to be experienced.

A questioning Latter Day Saint makes this observation, "We need the Spirit, but we need to expect in more advanced ways. As we progress, we are to expect 'pervasive inspiration.' This is above gifts and prophecy. On this level all are enlightened." And a hearer responds, "You mean these so-called spiritual gifts are to be outgrown?" A Latter Day Saint teen-ager confesses, "I've heard so much talk about the Holy Ghost, I'd like to find out what is real, if anything is, and what is just emotion." This kind of comment and concern could go on and on, with more diversity. Some observations would be cynical, but most would reflect the thinking of many honest members of the Church of Jesus Christ. There is great variety in the present-tense stock of interests and

14

reactions. These point up the sincere inquiry, "What is the Spirit?"

"Spiritual" Silence

Not much has been written and published about the Holy Spirit. Books on theology have had little, if anything, to say. Sometimes it appears that the subject is avoided. In the *Handbook of Christian Theology,* which came out a decade ago, Stanley Hopper made this forthright comment: "The doctrine of the Holy Spirit is at once the most central in the sense that everything in the Gospels is energized and motivated by and through its agency. The New Testament, as one commentator puts it, is preeminently the book of the Holy Spirit.... Yet, the doctrine has remained peripheral for the most part in the long history of doctrinal thinking" (page 170).

The historic creeds and confessions have been quite silent. The Apostles' Creed affirms, "I believe in the Holy Ghost." That is all. There were affirmations about believing in the "Holy Trinity," so something had to be said about the "Holy Ghost." In books about worship the Holy Spirit has had little mention. It was either ignored or taken for granted.

Two decades ago a book of some significance came out—*Spirit, Son, and Father* by Henry Van Dusen. The title itself was unusual. In earlier years it would have been "Father, Son, and Spirit." The subtitle was "Christian Faith in the Light of the Holy Spirit." In the foreword the author set forth his own experience, telling how the Holy Spirit was for him "a late discovery." He described his earlier impressions as "vague and unpleasant." His first source of difficulty was the term "Holy Ghost" that conveyed to him the feeling of something "misty, nebulous, ghostly, and unattractive." He went on to say that references to the Holy Ghost in hymns also contributed to his mood and his general dislike. Then he added, "In current Christian thought, there is wanting an adequate and convincing apprehension and appropriation of the Holy Spirit" (page 12).

Eventually Dr. Van Dusen began exploring. He found something stirring in "those conceptions of the Holy Spirit in which the New Testament is so rich" (page 9). This enabled him to put to the fore the need to get into the vital perception of this Spirit. His conclusion was, "A church devoid of a vital and vibrant possession by the Holy Spirit is a church congealed in ancient forms, or well on the way to spiritual sterility" (page 28). This daring statement is a call to exploration.

Reasons for Omissions

Here are some of the factors involved in these omissions concerning the Holy Spirit. They have varied from place to place, from time to time. Often these situations were not consciously created; they just evolved.

1. The Holy Ghost was considered something to be experienced, not examined. It was to speak for itself. Critical thinking was looked upon as hostile to and destructive of the expected experience.

2. The Holy Ghost was viewed as supernatural, so natural words would not apply. Man would not have

what would be needed for thinking about things in the world of the supernatural.

3. The person of genuine faith was not supposed to ask questions about such a holy matter. In prevailing notions of faith there is no place for doubt and inquiry. The slogan is "Only Believe!"

4. Hostility and heresy would be avoided by saying nothing about the Holy Ghost. By avoiding the total field there would be no misconceptions. The field was considered wide open for such confusions and such errors.

5. Other words could be used that would be safer—words that would take care of the matter with less confusion and speculation. Such a word was *grace.*

6. "Radical" movements often emphasized the expression of and possession by the Holy Ghost. These extreme expressions, notably of bodily form, sometimes came to be considered as "the way of the Spirit." Thus the Holy Spirit came to be discounted and often assigned to unwanted manifestations.

7. Church administrators became so involved in other fields of doctrine that they had little or no time or place for considerations of the Spirit. Thus the concern for and cultivation of the Holy Spirit was crowded out.

8. When administrators wanted to develop and maintain a centralized operation of a church, both in thinking and in operation, they could do so more effectively when they disregarded the "life of the Spirit." The person who advocated guidance by the Spirit tended to look directly to God rather than to church administrators. Persons "led by the Spirit" got

in the way with their individualistic interpretations and expressions.

9. Language was often lacking. Many had no thought-world for looking at and interpreting the life of the Spirit. The term "Holy Ghost" tended to get in the way. The language of the New Testament often was not meaningful in later centuries. It could be quoted, but quoting did not always carry meaning.

Assignment to the Supernatural

So often in religion we assign things to the supernatural. In general, this is thought of as denoting that which is "beyond nature" and cannot be interpreted and explained because it is "out there." It cannot be described in terms of natural law. This is well expressed in the *New Baltimore Catechism* of the Roman Catholic Church, where the Holy Ghost is designated as a member of "the Blessed Trinity" and as such is a supernatural mystery. Such a belief is to be accepted by the person on the authority of the church, through which comes "supernatural grace" by way of established channels. Such an approach makes a sharp line between what is natural, which is considered as examinable and interpretable, and what is supernatural and therefore a "divine mystery." What is more, it is not considered right for man to explore and examine what is supernatural.

Our exploration will avoid this dividing of reality into the natural and the supernatural. At one pole is what we can call the not-yet-understood; at the other, the quite-well-understood (but not *completely understood*—we cannot say this about anything). Between these two poles is a long range of perceiving. And the line between what we understand and what we do not understand is always moving. Things once assigned to the realm of the mysterious often move over to the world of the somewhat understood. Thus lightning, once assigned to the supernatural, is now recognized as natural phenomena. Tides, which were thought to be controlled by the whims of the gods of the ocean, are now linked to gravitational pull. So is it with many things. The line between somewhat-understood and the not-yet-understood keeps moving. And the line of the not-yet-understood keeps pushing out. We become more and more aware of things we never knew about—things both tangible and intangible.

Much of religion, including the Holy Spirit, has been assigned to the unknowable. More and more we are seeing this as something to be explained, to be considered in the laboratory of experience. What we often assigned to the "out there" can be regarded nondescribable because we do not have enough experience to do so. As we get into these areas we see how the phenomena are describable in terms of "natural law." And this applies to the Holy Spirit. We may be prekindergartners in experiencing and explaining it, but this does not warrant our saying that it is outside the realm of the explainable.

The Holy Spirit can be seen as God's way of functioning, and God's way is the natural way.

Confusion of Terms

In religion, as elsewhere, we are bothered to find words and phrases that express what we want to say.

19

Sometimes we do not give much attention to what we have in mind. Often we are tempted to use words that sound good but have little content. These may be referred to as "halo words." Thus "Holy Spirit," spoken fervently, can bring a glow of emotion but have little meaning.

An erstwhile pentecostal preacher testified of his "complete reliance on the Holy Ghost." Always he prayed "Give me the Holy Ghost!" but never did he ask for understanding or insight. He added that when he talked about the Holy Ghost, he never used words of his own—he had none. He always quoted from "the Word of God." He added that he might not know what it meant, but he knew that it was "the way God would say it, and had said it." He continued, "If we would only use God's words without being concerned about what they mean, we would get along better."

It is well to remember that God has to use the language available to him when he speaks to man. Jesus did this as he lived among his fellow Jews and spoke their words in ideas, in parables. So the language God uses will always be relative...and always incomplete. We are inclined to consider Scripture as the most meaningful phrasing available, and insist that it is complete and final. Often when something is written down, it is taken as the authoritative word.

Varied Terms for One Field

Through the centuries believers in God have tended to get hold of words or phrases and to tie them to something very specific. On the whole, God is not to be limited in this way. The honest person says that he is using the best wording available to him and hopes that he eventually may do better. The amateurs and the legalists often insist that there is one word for one expression and another word for another expression. They differentiate between "the Spirit of God" and "the Holy Ghost" and "the Holy Spirit," thus cutting up God's spiritual power into segments. Heated arguments have resulted. Through history these terms have been used to identify this universal spiritual reality. Some languages do not have adequate words, so the best terms available are used. This hair-splitting over terms has never been fruitful. Whatever term we use, it is never adequate for this great reality.

Here is instance of such definite distinctions. John A. Widstoe in his book, *Rational Theology*, makes a sharp distinction between the Holy Ghost and the Holy Spirit: "The chief agent employed by God to communicate his will to the universe is the holy spirit, which must not be confused with the Holy Ghost, the personage who is the third member of the Godhead" (page 68). "The holy spirit permeates all the things of the universe, material and spiritual. . . . By the intelligent domination and infinite extent of the holy spirit, the whole universe is held together and made a whole." He says that the Holy Spirit "fills every person" enabling each to communicate with God. This, he notes, bears a sharp distinction from the Holy Ghost. "God, the Holy Ghost, is a personage of spirit, who possesses special functions which have not been clearly revealed." He continues by saying that the gift of the Holy Ghost is available through the rite of the laying on of hands after baptism. This segmentizes God's empowering of man.

Some day we should have more adequate words, clearer concepts to indicate the nature and the functioning of this divine power. We shall do well to avoid this sectioning of this spiritual ministering by designating different functions and realities that we call by different names. One conscientious man, perplexed by the arguments for different names, dropped them all and merely spoke of "the Good Spirit." He was trying.

Original Words

Biblical writers used the most meaningful terms available to them. Sometimes they must have felt like the small boy who saw a giraffe the first time. He said to himself, "There can't be any name for it." He did not deny that he saw something, but he couldn't label it.

The Hebrews in ancient times used the word *ruach* (literally "breath") to indicate "spirit." It meant to them the life-giving breath of God. So they wrote how God formed man out of "the dust of the ground" and then breathed into him "the breath of life" (Genesis 2:8). This terminology carried through the Old Testament, and Dr. Van Dusen observed that it always denoted two qualities, *intimacy* and *potency*. God gave power to man and was near to him personally.

The New Testament writers used two Greek words when they spoke of the Spirit: they used *dynamis* to express spiritual power. They took it from the world of physical power. "Dynamo" in the English language was adapted from this term. They also used the word *pneuma*, which literally meant "spirit," and preceded it with "holy" to designate divine quality. The Book of Acts records the coming of "the Spirit" upon the Gentiles; the words *pneuma* and *agion* are used (11:15).

Many translators regret that "pneuma" came to be translated as "ghost." This came to convey a mood and a meaning that often diverted from the basic meaning. This misapplication is expressed in the comment of the little girl who wanted to go to prayer meeting on Halloween so she could get "the Holy Ghost." It is expedient to avoid this word in cultures in which ghostly spirits have a place. We shall do well to search for the meaning that best denotes both what the Spirit is and what it is for.

Need to Explore

Socrates is credited with saying, "The unexamined life is not worth living." He meant something more than dissecting life in a take-things-apart treatment. He spoke of life in a continuing way. He never withdrew from life in order to do an encyclopedic treatment of it. He did his examining during the process of living. He never put persons on an exhibit table to peer at them; he lived with them. He kept asking, "Who are you?" "Where are you going?" "And for what?"

I would add this comment: "The unexamined religion is dangerous." It can sink into magic and superstition. It can narrow our living; it can build up

23

fences that shut us in. It can cause us to look at things quite otherwise than they are in the universe. Yes, some expressions of religion can make us narrow, self-centered, lazy. There has been much of this kind of religion through the centuries. Some see it and think this is all there is to religion. A farmer said of a visitor to his farm, "He got stuck with some cockleburrs and acted as if they were all that was out there. He never saw the woods and the cornfields." Many persons look at religion and make this sort of evaluation. And there is much of this in the realm of the Holy Spirit. Strange things are assigned to it. A person with only a partial view can see a wild, exotic shouting group in action and conclude that he has seen the manifestation of the Spirit.

This affirmation about examining religion does not hold up examination as the main thing to be sought. It is not the essence of religion, but it *is* an essential part. Reading textbooks on dietetics alone will not provide the nourishment we need, but it can help us provide a health-affording pattern of eating. The same principle applies to spiritual food. Yet often we need to study guide texts on spiritual food.

Unsound Examination

These are instances out of the book of life. Here are persons who thought it right to believe but wrong to examine their beliefs. This would constitute lack of faith, in their thinking. A man—we shall call him Bill—believed that it was God's will that he read the Bible and memorize passages so he might guide others. He was never to think of the morrow; he was never to be concerned with "mammon." So he sat in his rocking chair reading and waiting for God to send somebody with groceries for him. He read how the Holy Ghost had come to those who "truly trusted" and considered what he was doing as the approved way to bring to pass spiritual endowment. And his notions were so much prompted by God, as he saw them, that they must never be called in question. When neighbors suggested that he get a job and earn his "board and keep," he felt that their counsel smacked of lack of faith.

A middle-aged man said that the Spirit told him to move to Independence, Missouri, and to refrain from working. The end of the world was near, and God would provide him with necessities for living. He also said the Spirit advised him to refrain from bathing, for if he did he would be aping worldly ways with fragrant soaps. This would be bowing to comfort, to transitory values of the passing age. Since the Spirit told him to do these things, they were not to be questioned. The outcome of his course of action was not good for health, for harmony, for happiness. His notions about the Holy Spirit needed examining ever so much.

Explore, Experiment, Exercise

Alma, a prophet of ancient America provided some sound counsel: "Awake and arouse your faculties!" (Alma 16:151). He told his people to "experiment" and to "exercise." They were to "nourish the seed they had planted with great care." And when they did this they would be able to say, "This begins to enlarge my soul;

25

this begins to enlighten my understanding" (16:154). This was exploring of the first rank.

Nothing in God's universe is too sacred for examination. If the exploration is well timed and well conducted, insight and inspiration will result. God intends people to grow in spiritual competency so they will be qualified to examine and explore and this applies to the Holy Spirit. To qualify they must build up funds of spiritual living that will give them something to work with. An empty-life person, charged with cynicism, emptiness, negativism, and self-centeredness, will hardly have anything to examine. He would not know how to distinguish what is spiritual. A wise Saint observed, "One never finds out what love is if all he does is read psychological treatises and study personality rating tests." And he was right. Then he added, "The person who oozes sentiment will not know what love is either."

Something as essential as the Holy Spirit calls for first-class exploration. And this will occur in the laboratory of living, where the explorer is giving honest effort to getting with the spiritual reality he calls the Holy Spirit.

Personhood

Is

Foremost

"Let's suppose that you were God and that you were going to do some creating. You were just starting out and you were planning what to do. What would you create first? And what would you give high place in all your creating?" a teacher asked a circle of junior boys and girls.

One boy said, "I think I would want to practice up a bit before I did the main job." Another said, "I would want to do some big things, such as making a mountain or an ocean. After I started on them, I could just keep piling up. Then I'd go to the complicated job."

"And what would you consider the most complicated job?" queried the teacher. The answer was immediate: "Making a man!" Then the teacher asked why that would be complicated. One boy spoke up, "Because we are so mixed up and often so bullheaded." Another junior spoke up, "I do not mean making just a two-legged animal. I mean making a person who can think and do other things that no other animal can do." A junior philosopher said, "Yes, man is the biggest risk in all creation." And another added, "I would never be sure how man would turn out. God might have one idea about what man is to be, but man might get some crazy notion of his own."

Eventually a boy made this observation, "Things might have been more certain for God if he had worked out some sort of mechanical man that could be put together and wound up. Then man would have to go the way God wanted him to go." Another responded, "I think God wanted something more than a machine. I think he wanted something that could love him and would also want to be loved." The teacher gave them the word "robot," and they grabbed on to it. "I would rather be a person than a pig or a monkey or a robot," one affirmed. Then came the question: "Just what is man? What makes him more than a pig or a monkey or a machine?" These junior searchers were positing something pretty important: man stands foremost in God's creating.

An Enduring Question

A lad asked his mother, "What am I?" His mother thought a moment and then said, "Bobby, you're a person." Then he asked, "What's a person?" The mother hesitated a while and then started, "A person, you know a person is...." Fortunately the telephone rang and she was delivered. As she started for the telephone, she continued, "We'll talk about this later." Bobby did not get help in finding the answer. We wonder what the mother would have said to him as she endeavored to identify what a person is. How would she have spoken meaningfully to him?

A sound, functional identification of what constitutes being a person is at the heart of our exploration of what God is. Lazy thinking will not do. Quotations out of Scriptures will not speak adequately to most junior inquirers. . .or older ones either. We need to get right to the business of exploring what is involved in becoming a person.

We wonder what further questions Bobby might ask. He might ask, as other children have, "Is God a person too?" Once a boy saw a mongoloid child in church. Perplexed, he asked, "Is he a person or something else?" Later he asked, "What is the difference between him and me?" In time he continued, "Could he be baptized or would he know enough to be?" And a boy with affection for his dog inquired, "Could my dog receive the Holy Spirit?" Bobby's question stands: "What is a person?"

Historic Background

This word "person" goes back to the days of the Greek Theater. The actor would put on a mask to indicate the kind of role he was playing. The two general groups were tragedy and comedy, but there were others too. The Latins took over this notion of the mask for the actor. It is thought that the word "person" came from combining the prefix *per-* which expresses "through" with the syllable "son" which came from the Latin word for "sound." The mask had a large opening for the mouth so the actor would be able to "sound through" and be heard.

At first the word *persona* referred to the mask, and then it came to refer to the person on the inside who wore the mask. It meant playing a role, and it also meant interaction with others when speaking in that role. Our conception of "person" was not the same as in the ancient world of thinking. There were two aspects of this early functioning of the *persona* that continued: (1) the inside character who was to "speak through" and (2) the impression made on those outside. Usually the emphasis was on the latter. In today's society this often tends to be the emphasis. Often there is less concern with the "real stuff" on the inside than with the facade that impresses those on the outside.

Present Meaning

A much-used word can gather many meanings and moods, and we shall do well to ask one another, "Just what do you mean when you use that word?" "Person" is one of those words with varied meanings in different categories (psychology, sociology, anthropology, education, religion, advertising, etc.). From it has come the word "personality." Hawkers of products, salesmen for cults of beliefs and behaviors, advocates for social climbing, and more have grabbed hold of this word. Often it is used loosely and cheaply.

Yes, the meaning of "person" has developed fairly recently. Now we think of "personhood" as a creation that comes to pass after the birth of a baby. Now we say that a person is born a candidate to become human. And we add that this will happen to the degree the infant has the natural equipment to live in person-to-person relationship with others. (A baby may be born so deficient in native powers that he cannot become a person. Or, after birth, he may not have the quality of association with others that is required for achieving personhood.)

A parent-to-be commented, "This comprehension of what it means to become a person places a heavy responsibility on us parents and on all who have anything to do with the child. It is up to us to enable this creation of ours to become a person." True, this is a "heavy responsibility," but it should not be regarded with a sense of oppression or depression. It is an opportunity for creative expression calling for wisdom, faith, hope, and mutual enterprise. Every time a new candidate is born, we are called to assist in developing personhood of worthful quality.

This conception of personhood is one of the great ideas of modern life. It can be twisted for shallow purpose or elevated for developing persons of "eternal quality." It is at the heart of religion. It is basic in interpreting the Holy Spirit.

Core of Personhood

Personhood is something to be experienced. It cannot be looked at and measured and touched, but it is real.

Let us think of *person* as a man—whatever age, whichever sex—who has developed qualities that distinguish him from the animal. As he becomes a person, he distinguishes between what is "out there" and what is "in here." A mother said, "It was a great moment when Jackie realized that his toe and his finger were his own, that they were different from the bed and the chair." Jackie was starting to become a person. We call this distinguishing his own "self."

Three basics take place in the development of selfhood: self-awareness, self-identification, and self-management. This personhood may be shallow, or simple, but it is a start.

The philosopher Fichte observed that the moment when a child thinks and says "I" for the first time he has come to a new birth—a birth as important as the biological one. Here the child is beginning to take an attitude toward this "self" of his. The concept may be fuzzy, but there is reality in it.

What expandable possibilities throughout life are reflected in these expressions of personhood—self-awareness, self-identification, and self-management! The person may be thwarted by inadequate patterns of living, of looking at himself, or he may grow with ever enlarging notions of personhood and how to realize these. The person can include God in his development or leave God out. And he can include God with sound or unsound patterns. What he does about Deity can narrow or expand his personhood.

Meaning of Personality

This word *personality* basically refers to the qualities of a person that distinguish him from other persons. It is a matter of identity. Ideas and interests condition what observers pick out for distinguishing and rating each person. They may look at the way a person talks, walks, or "gawks." In so doing they disclose which things mean most and attract most.

We need some sound terms for describing wholeness in persons and designating worthful personality. Often we do not take a complete look. We pick out a few qualities because they make an impression on others. If we like these qualities, then the person we observe is likely to be labeled as having approved personality. One young woman commented, "I like the way he holds his cigarette." Another said, "I like the rhythm in his dancing." Still another observed, "I like the size of his billfold." Every person is measured by the kind of qualities by which he identifies others as to "personality." Jesus had his estimates for "abundant living." He never stooped to prevailing pictures of popular personality.

Helen Keller

This is a story of the achieving of personhood. It began in March 1887, just before Helen was seven years of age. Annie Sullivan came to the Keller home in Alabama to begin setting free the spirit of a girl who was blind and deaf and did not speak—the result of a serious illness when she was nineteen months old. Annie first referred to her pupil as "the little savage," but she persisted in trying to communicate by touch. The first association recorded was when Miss Sullivan pumped some cold water on Helen's hand and spelled out w-a-t-e-r several times by touching the small hand. On the way back to the house Helen was excited and sought to learn the names of other objects. In a few hours she had learned thirty words. It was a momentous day for both pupil and teacher. That night the formerly obstreperous girl crawled in bed with her teacher and kissed her. Then came lessons in speaking. It was a great day when Helen could say falteringly, "I-am-not-dumb-now." In time she learned to say such words as mother and father and teacher. She was finding relationship. She was developing personhood.

Helen Keller pushed out more and more. The personal relationship she had established with her teacher and family was extended. God came into her world of persons, and she came to refer to her faith in her "Divine Friend." She affirmed that those who are blind put their hand in God's hand. The emergence of Helen Keller from isolation to personal relationship is a revelation to the world.

Freedom for Personhood

Personhood requires freedom. Without ability and disposition and setting to choose freely man cannot live as a person. If biological drives dominate, he is an animal. If domineering management controls, he is a slave. If passing whims direct, he is a jumping toy, wound up by passing appeals. If fear of God impels, he is a dumb devotee. Personalism calls for "the power of self-determination." Man has to have what it takes to manage himself. This involves a wide range of factors and functions.

Often we are inclined to think of freedom in terms of getting rid of felt pressure or police power. We think that if we could be released from some specific force we would be free. Not so. We could be released from one factor, such as requirement to get in at curfew time, and then be enslaved by another controlling force, such as liquor or drugs or financial enslavement.

We can also be slaves to our prejudices. Freedom is an inclusive operation. A trackster who ran the quarter-mile was invited to a drinking party one night. He said he was not free to do so. His friends asked him what he meant. "If I take the liberty to drink, I'll lose my liberty to run." Freedom always includes freedom *for* something as well as freedom *from* something. The person who manages well looks to major freedom in the perspective of his total personhood.

Divergent Views

In some religions man is held up as worthful. In some he is a pawn to serve and entertain the gods. In some he is merely to be "put up with." In others he is regarded as somebody who "got fouled up" and dropped down to low estate. In still others he is told of the hopeful state of things at a coming time when he will lose consciousness and have no personal identity; whatever he has been will flow into the great ocean of reality.

Some religionists describe man as a clod, some as a worm, some as a beast. Others elevate him to a pedestal and picture a world in which everything is intended to give him whatever he wants. Others picture him as "teacher's pet." Many think of him as intended to be "perfect" and to be eternally "saved," but without the ability to do anything about it. In his native state he has little or no self-management. He is to "surrender" and have God do all the saving. This is hardly a self-managing person.

Among the first questions we need to ask about a religion are, "What is the nature of man? Is he considered worthful? What kind of person is he to be? How are man and God going to get together in this person-with-person relationship? What is the function of the Holy Spirit in all this?"

The Hebrew Faith

The book of Genesis opens with a high declaration about man. It affirms that God said, "Let us make man in our own image." God is designated as breathing into man "the breath of life" and assigning him the managing of his own living. Man was to take the consequences of his choices. If he mischose, he would incur ill effects. And if he chose wisely there would be good returns both in his own life and in the lives of others.

The Psalmist sang, "What is man that thou art mindful of him?" This was not a discounting of man. Rather was there the implication that God had rated man pretty high and was continuing to do so, although God was often disappointed with the way man managed his living.

Something vital is said in the Book of Ezekiel. The author was a young exile in Babylon. He had been taken there in the first deportation of Jews about 597 B.C. God had something for him to do; he was to be a prophet among his people there and get them to sense the mission God had for them—to hold true and return, in time, to their own city, Jerusalem. Chapter Two contains the story of God's calling of Ezekiel. Ordinarily in those days when a man came into the presence of God, it was thought that he should fall down, signifying his unworthiness. God said to

Ezekiel, "Son of man, stand upon your feet, and I will speak to you." God wanted him to stand up with square shoulders, with eye to the fore, with chin up, and listen to the charge that he was going to receive. God was forthright. He told Ezekiel that he was going to have an exacting assignment that would require courage and stamina, but God also said that he need not be afraid, for He would be right there with him. Here was a high trust in man.

This same relationship is expressed in God's calling Moses to return to Egypt and deliver the Hebrews. Moses' reaction was, "Who am I, that I should do work like this?" (Exodus 3:10). God helped him to have confidence. A later conference between God and Moses is related in Section 22 of Doctrine and Covenants. The charge came directly, "I have a work for you Moses, my son." Then God gave him a survey view of his creative program, so Moses would be able to work with understanding. God was thinking of man as a son, not a slave. God wanted Moses to understand so he would be able to speak understandingly to his people.

Jesus and Persons

Jesus' ministry was directed toward helping persons have the "abundant" life. One day the Pharisees reproved him and his disciples for going through the fields and plucking grain on the Sabbath day. To them the main thing was observing Sabbath according to prescribed regulations. The disciples obviously were hungry and took some grain for food. There was no complaint about stealing, and eating grain in this way was quite all right in Jewish life. But it was not to be done on the Sabbath, for this constituted working. Jesus' response was direct: "The Sabbath was made for man and not man for the Sabbath" (Mark 2:25). He placed the welfare of man to the fore. Institutions were to help men live the good life as sons of God.

After Jesus left earth, this conception of man continued for a while. Then, in the thinking of many, a lower conception prevailed. Man was thought of as having lost the ability to want to do good. He was considered helpless in his depraved condition. God had to do everything. In fact, all men were bound for hell. In the doctrine of "election" certain men were chosen to be saved—not that they merited salvation but that God might have them to worship and glorify him. The lost ones had no right to complain. In this picture man was hardly a person. A person has the ability to make choices, to manage his course.

In this fallen state man was designated as "natural"—animalistic, self-centered, and anti-spiritual. Only God could save him. Today there are two contrasting meanings of the term "natural man." The conventional meaning in Scriptures is sensuous, depraved, without goodness. The other meaning, which is used in science, designates the total equipment with which man is born. This is descriptive rather than evaluative. And there are several theories about the original nature of man.

Throughout this exploration the word "natural" will be used to designate "original." This will convey that the nature of man, as designated by Deity, is for achieving personhood of quality worthy to be with

God. When man gets separated from God he lives below his potentials. The natural way, intended by God, is for man to utilize divine resources that will enable him to develop personhood with eternal quality.

Personhood to the Fore

Let us ask, "What is the most important thing in our lives? What do we rate highest in our universe?" Answers will vary. In some places the state is foremost; man is a mere servant to the political order. In some, the military is supreme. A recent revolutionist said that only two things talk—guns and bombs. In some situations social standing is considered most important. The main thing is to "keep up with the Joneses" and, if possible, to get ahead of them. In some societies economic production and prosperity are thought of as foremost. Advocates hold that if man aims first at economic production all other things will come. There are social groups in which the major interest is a whing-ding high life designed to combat monotony and boredom. Others will insist that the main thing in life is sex satisfaction. Sometimes the continuing of the family name is the main concern. The list could be expanded.

Among churches there is wide range in the estimating of what ranks highest. One man says, "The Bible, the Word of God, is everything." He believes that if he has this, he has everything he needs. Another says that celestial glory ranks above all else. Another asserts that the foremost thing is baptism of the Holy Ghost. Others set forth numerical increase in converts as the indication of "spiritual success." Others measure in terms of financial income and church wealth. For many disciples the major concern is in "sharing the good news" with others that they may be "lifted and leavened" thereby.

In God's program of living the most worthful thing is the *person*. This involves persons as they are and persons as they are going to become. Gerald Kennedy in *I Believe* wrote, "The Christian view of life is based on the belief that persons are worth more than anything else" (page 70). Jesus asserted this, lived it, and commissioned his followers to minister with this conviction.

Yes, personhood is foremost. This affirmation is inclusive. It refers to every person in every land, in every culture. It refers to children, youth, adults. It includes both sexes and those who are confused about their own natures. It includes all generations—those who lived centuries ago and those who will be living in the future. It includes those who have lived commendable lives and those who have muddled up their living. It includes all religious groupings. The salutation, "Our Father," is designed to have universal and eternal application. God puts personhood to the fore.

We inquire how God and man are going to have personal relationship. God invites us to explore. This is the field of the ministering of the Holy Spirit.

Persons
Live In
Relationships

There is no such thing as an "atomistic" person. This phrase denotes one who lives apart, without any communication, without any relationship to others. But, simply stated, "There is no such animal." The person comes to be and continues in personal relationships, both direct and indirect.

Some years ago a term, "feral man," was coined to designate one who has lived apart from others. There were a few cases in which a child had survived in what was considered general apartness. Sometimes the survival was through the help of other animals. Sometimes the isolation took place through some unusual notions of adults. But these "ferals" could hardly be called persons. In the main, they lacked the essentials of personhood. They lacked concepts of thinking. They lacked means for communicating thought. And after they had lived so long in this condition their bodies and habits were pretty much set against any possibilities of personal development.

Occasionally some person will become weary of "the world" and decide to withdraw into comparative solitude. Such a person, however, takes with him the heritage and achievements of his world. While alone he lives with persons of former ages. Once a recluse chose to live apart in his own cottage, avoiding communication with other living persons. But on his table was his well-worn Bible through which he associated with ever so many acquaintances. He was dwelling with their reflections, their experiences, their revelations. And in his library were copies from Plato to William James. In his garden were rosebushes that some specialists had created. And he grew tomatoes that came out of advanced civilization. He would read Scriptures aloud in the language of his own people. He was far from being an "atomistic" monk.

Interpersonal Relationships

The person emerges through interpersonal relationships and stays a person through these continuing relationships. He grows well through some, decreases through others. He becomes stunted if he is deprived of relationships with persons of merit. A man disgusted with happenings in the world lamented, "There is no way for me to resign from the human race." When a friend suggested that he might go to some far-off wilderness away from human habitation, he responded with a sense of realism, "And who would I get with out there? Crows and chipmunks?" After a moment he added, "If I stay here I'll clash with the human nuts; if I go out there I shall clunk with the other nuts." His human reactions would continue.

Man is born a candidate to become a person. He does not arrive ready-made in personalism. If the infant were aware of this, he would likely experience satisfaction and dissatisfaction about the company of persons into which he was born. And his wish might well be, "May I have the kind of relationships with the kind of persons who will enable me to be a real somebody." The infant does not know all this. Often adults do not know this. Many times a baby is only something to cuddle and carry the name of the parents. The kinds of persons with whom this candidate lives make tremendous difference. One youth said frankly, "If when I was born, I had had the chance to choose, I would have selected a different group of persons for my family and my community and my church. But I had to take what I inherited." Then he smiled and said, "I have learned to do the most with what I have. Some of it is pretty good. Now maybe I can help them a little."

When Arnold Toynbee surveyed history he wrote this summary statement: "Man is neither a selfless ant nor an unsocial cyclops but a social animal, whose personality can be expressed and developed only through relations with other personalities" (*A Study of History*, Volume II of Abridgement, page 79). He was saying that to become and be a person man has to live with others. As he does so a network of relationships results.

It is said that a man has developed a self when he can look at his own stock of experiences and say, "This is Me." As Dr. Herbert Meade used to say he comes to say, "I looks at me." His notion of his self will be incomplete, immature, but he has "something" that constitutes a distinctive awareness. Other persons become a mirror in which he can look at himself. It marks personal accomplishment when a wee one can get hold of his toe and say, "This is my toe." It is a further accomplishment when he can say in substance, "This is my idea." In *A Return to Vision*, the three authors, Cherry, Conley, and Hirsch put it this way, "As a human being, [man] established identity through relationships to things outside of himself" (page 1). These things range from friends and family members to patterns of thinking to social usages in the social world. And the physical world is included. All these things enable the beginning person to sense that he is somebody, with his own self. And the world of relationships is to keep pushing out. And God gets in this world of relationships.

The Problem of Identity

This interaction with other persons, directly and indirectly, functions in helping the individual to arrive at some idea of who he is. Occasionally this social interaction may confuse the person with respect to his identity. He may misread and misinterpret his experiences. The classic example is Willie Loman in *Death of a Salesman*. When Willie Loman died, his son was described as saying of him, "He never knew who he was." Elsewhere Loman was described as being primarily concerned with the externals that society imposed, the externals that would enable him to "go over big." So his marks became a smile and a shoeshine. The smile was practiced for effect. The shoeshine was ever maintained. Many are like Willy Loman: they do not have any clear, consistent notion as to who they are and what they are for.

This problem of identity is increasing because society has become so mobile and the tempo of change has speeded up. Communication media have given so much, with such complexity, that many people have difficulty "putting things together." A modern commentator can say, "Today the sense of self is deficient."

Concerned youth are asking, "Who am I? Where am I going? What is the meaning of life?" Rollo May writes in *Psychology and the Human Dilemma* that the problem of identity has become "the crisis of the loss of the sense of significance" (page 26). He adds that today many are inclined to say, "I may not know who I am, but at least I can make them notice me." This was expressed by the leader of a campus revolt at the University of California at Berkeley in his comment that members of his group were resisting the "facelessness of students in the modern factory university." Another spoke of trends in our socio-economic life toward making persons "anonymous cogs in the wheels of a tremendous system." Dr. Clark Kerr, president of the university, observed that the students "wanted to be treated as distinct individuals." A factory worker commented that he did not want to work at a machine so that he would be made over into its image.

All this is saying that the emerging person wants to be somebody with a distinctive self. He wants a sense of worth. He wants a conviction of significance. He wants a chance to choose what he does. Such a person wants a religion that enables him to be a worthful person.

More Than Popular Personality

The sound person stands on his feet, among his peers and contemporaries, as a total self. In popular usage the word "personality" tends to apply to socially observable, socially oriented aspects of behavior. Here concern is with impression on others. In this sense we may hear, "She has a pleasing personality" or "He needs to do something to improve his personality!" It is this outer layer of the person that the so-called charm schools seek to enhance. We need to guard against the assumption that some superficial aspects of personality reveal the "real person." And we need to be aware that some persons live in worlds with different patterns and values and never achieve oneness. Some put up curtains that cover the true self. What genuine study is concerned with is the "real" person—with a stock of values, with a pattern of interaction that carries on consistently. The wobbling person lacks this consistency in values, in patterns of relating, in evaluation of himself.

A Matter of Values

Animals do not have values; they do what is biologically satisfying. Bears do not have a conference and decide that it will be to their advantage to take a long winter sleep; they hibernate instinctively. A mother pig does not attend a class on population control and decide whether to have more piglets.

Instincts take their course. But in the interaction of persons there emerges the view that some things have priority in the scale of worth. The choice may be sound or otherwise. Persons can become troubled when their values get confused or endangered. A man in western United States confessed, "If I lose my land—and it looks as if I am going to—what have I to live for?" Here his land stood for much more than money value. It stood for joy in growing things. It brought him close to plains and to mountains. Here he could have solitude in open country. Here his family lived. Many values were caught up in his homestead land.

Dr. Rollo May points up the need for continuing values in the healthy person. When he wrote about the turmoil in contemporary student life, he said it is "the inner experience of values" that provides the "core" around which the youth knows himself as a person. It is this core of values that gives him "something to commit himself to." It does not mean holding to something that is worn out, that belongs to another day. It does involve using the heritage of former days in present evaluation. When values go, the person gets confused or internally divided or rebellious or apathetic.

Chain Reaction

The world of a person reaches out in chain reaction. What he does has far-reaching effect, and what others do affects him. This exploration is built on the previously stated belief that persons are of more worth than anything else. In *I Believe* Gerald Kennedy says,

"Each man's life, yours, mine, any man's, is of lasting value." To this is added the affirmation, "We are made to live together." This is more than gregarious mingling, more than a classification of human beings in groups and social registers, more than quoting "God is love." This is a living together with the appreciation of every person in his own right. It includes the life-span from infancy through sunset years—persons as they are and as they may become, for better or for worse.

This puts to the fore consideration of the kind of persons God has designed that his children be. It includes the resources he has provided for this purpose. It involves the ministering of the Holy Spirit in bringing to pass persons who get together with eternal values uniting and motivating them.

Today we are "one world" more than ever before in regard to interaction. It is said that during the recent half century we have rocketed through more change in more fields than in the previous two million years. There is more interinfluence among the three billion people on earth today than ever before. In 1492, when the Western Hemisphere was discovered, the peoples of Europe were not affected by those who lived in Siberia, Tahiti, Peru, or Nigeria. Today things are different. What affects one segment of humanity affects others. A crop failure in India has far-reaching effect. The extension of Marxist philosophy and practice in Southeast Asia brings repercussions in many places. A tragedy in the Olympics stirs every continent.

The kind of relationship makes a difference. It is not

enough that persons from here and there shall meet. How they meet and interact matters very much. This is illustrated by what has happened in Africa during the past four centuries. Once Europeans and Asiatics went to Africa to grab men and carry them into slavery. Once whites went in as grabbing imperialists. Once missionaries went in as condescending preachers to invite "the heathen" to accept the white man's way of believing and living. Now whites and browns and yellows go in and live alongside Africans with appreciation of the "African personality." They go with expectation that these blacks can teach them something about establishing a soulful relationship with the land. They can hear the chieftain say that the European and American speak of what they *have* while the African and his land speak of what *is*.

The kind of relationship matters much.

Interinfluence of Persons

While in Greece Paul of Tarsus wrote a letter to the congregation of Christians at Rome telling of his hope to come there. He also expressed his desire to move on to Spain. In this letter Paul sensed how human beings have to have something worthful to live for. He set forth that man needs to get with and draw on something larger, more lasting than himself, and this is God. He pictured a personal God wanting men to have right relationships with one another and with him. He wrote how this continuing purpose, this inclusive work of God lifts above triviality and insignificance. And he saw how when men really relate to God they also relate to other persons.

Paul declared this interrelationship of persons in this terse sentence: "None of us lives to himself and none of us dies to himself" (Romans 14:7). He might have said his conviction this way, "Men are united in Christ." This was his message: Men are bonded together in mutuality as they are all living in disciple relationship with Christ. He wrote that men need this unity in Christ in order to live together in ongoing relationship. This was to be seen as a constructive, creative expression in brotherly relationship. The saints were to work at achieving right relationship. Later in his letter he wrote, "let us then pursue the things that make for peace, things wherewith one may edify another" (Romans 14:19). Another translation makes this word "edify" read "mutual upbuilding." Sometimes this word "edify" is made to carry the connotation of a warm, emotional glow. This is good, but this is not enough. When we remember that the words edify and ediface come from the same root, we can sense the active building up that is involved. This relating to Christ, this relating to others is an active, well-directed living together.

Physical Environment

The kind of physical environment makes a difference. The way man reacts to and manages his environment is of utmost consequence. There are three main attitudes: (1) that the physical environment controls us, (2) that this environment conditions us, (3) that this environment makes no difference. In the main, the second of these will stand forth as chosen in this exploration: the kind of physical setting makes a difference—but not an all-determining difference. What man does with his physical environment makes a great difference. Eskimos do not raise beds of lilies. The Africans do not build snowmen. The list could go on and on. Men are conditioned but need not be controlled.

How persons relate to their environment makes a difference in their values. Some think of themselves associating in a spiritual way with the nature in which they live. Mount Fujiyama draws and speaks to native Japanese. Some think of their land and its bounties as a stewardship entrusted to them to take care of and maintain. Some think of physical resources as means for adding to their own personal wealth and social standing. The driving rule is "Get it before someone else gets it." Some consider that everything is to be left without human interference or change: no dams are to be built; no irrigation ditches are to be dug; no trees are to be cut. To do any of these things would be meddling with the way God put things together. Some think of natural resources as belonging to the group, not to the individual. In this case there are no individual titles, and decisions about the resources are made by the group.

How man relates to his physical environment conditions what he is going to do, how much time and energy he is going to devote to these resources. To understand the religion of persons or peoples, one must discover their notions and values about their physical environment. This involves how they view God in relation to the whole—which involves ideas about the Holy Spirit.

51

Community Influence

Community that engenders wholesome personhood is more than gregariousness. The mere putting of persons together may make for shallowness, for stratified society, for social conflict, for impersonalized relationships. The kind of society must be developed that will further the realization of wholesome selfhood. This includes the family, school, community, church, and government. In the society most contributive to personhood, there is awareness that the kind of person wanted and realized makes a difference. Everyone is viewed as somebody who counts for something.

In such a community the worth of a person is indicated in terms of what he is doing for the total good. He is sanctioned to the degree that he (1) discovers his potential, (2) develops it, (3) devotes it to the longtime good of all, and (4) delights in doing this. It is imperative to consider what kind of community will do this. One youth set forth his wants quite definitely. He wanted to be a gold-digger, a car-dragger, and a girl-dumper. His name was Bill—King William the Only. Everything centered in him, in his wants at the given moment. When he confronted William the Other, whose values and patterns were like his own, the war was on. They had no disposition to cooperate with each other. One had to win—and William the Only did. Both became victims to their way of living.

It takes the right kind of community to develop genuine personhood. The development of a self of worth requires interaction with other selves. And the quality of relationship with these other selves is of great consequence. Such interaction can vary from a stifling, narrowing experience to an expanding, ennobling relationship.

Importance of Language

In the formative stages of personhood development and all through life language is the passport for making contact. We need it for self-discovery, for self-identification. This language is more than verbal. We speak with our whole selves. The first language of the child is gesture and action. Originally this may be for spontaneous expression, for body satisfaction. These gestures and actions come to mean something to others, and then to the child. Communication has started. Sometimes language may function as a toy as well as a means of communication for a child. This can happen in an adult too. He may seem to be saying, "I have nothing to say, but I find it satisfying to hear myself talk." Largely, however, language is for communication, and this is basic in the emergence and continuing development of selfhood.

Much of the time in our Western society we have been inclined to act as if verbal language is the *one* form—or at least the highest form—of communication. A vocabulary is not to be discounted, but we must not give spoken words a monopoly. During recent years we have been coming to see that a person speaks with his total self. In a congregation in the Netherlands the members said of one minister, "He talks all over." They watched his face. They noted the intonation of his voice. They observed his gestures.

Then they waited for the translator to put the speaker's English into Dutch. Yes, the highly communicative person talks all over.

It has been said that linguistically man is not born free. He is conditioned by the language he inherits. Words carry meanings and moods. They carry a history of experience. And the language into which a man is born may be rich or limited. The Tahitian language is richer in specifics than in abstract concepts. The Greek language has three words to express types of love—biological, social, and spiritual —while English is limited to one.

It has been observed that we do not live in the midst of the whole world but only in the part of it that our language lets us know. Language reveals our views about our world, about ourselves, about our total environment. Language helps to shape our ideas as well as affording expression of them. This calls for us to keep expanding our experience so our language will increase. And the increasing language will make possible an increase of experience. There is much more to expanding our vocabulary than learning words. And this applies to expanding our living with God.

An effective relationship calls for language that speaks for the whole person and keeps increasing contact with the total world in which the person lives. This also applies to relating with God and the Holy Spirit.

Relationship with God

The total person is to be visioned as reaching out in continuing, expanding relationship with the wholeness of God in the fullness of the universe. Less than this is cutting short the resources available for personhood development. The creative, exploring person will keep at the job, trying for an enriched and enriching relationship with spiritual resources. The honest person will see his concepts of God calling for growth and refinement. He will see his language needing expansion. He will see conventional ways of getting with God as not adequate. He will see that many who set out to relate with God have limiting notions. But the person of pioneering spirit will thrill at the great adventure in relating more and more.

And the Holy Spirit will minister in this exploration. The true outreacher will endeavor to see how this Spirit calls for right relationship.

Living
Requires
Resources

"Resource" is more than an ordinary word. It has origin and history that carry significance. The prefix *re* means "again." The major part of the word comes from the Latin verb which carries the idea of rising or lifting up. The word has come to mean a source of supply for enabling something to be carried on. If a person has resources, he is supposed to be able to "do the job." This mood of the word implies continuing availability and utility.

Required Resources

Living requires resources. A first question we ask about a planet other than earth is "Does life exist there?" We wonder whether there is enough oxygen for breathing, the right temperature for human existence, and so on. In the light of lack of resources for living on other planets, a usually grumpy man commented, "It's a pretty good earth we have. We need to appreciate it more." Then he added, "It takes something to be able to live."

Resources are not uniform all around our planet. Conditions in some locations are more conducive to healthful living than those in some other parts, and different individuals may require different settings. One person's state of health and biological qualities may keep him from surviving in a region where another may get along fairly well. (This can apply to thinness of the air, temperature, humidity, particulates, plant and animal life.) Allergies can annoy and even bring illness. The soil may be more or less suited for furnishing food. Living on this planet requires right resources of several kinds.

There is more to living than biological existence, of course. This is not discounting the physical aspects of living. It is saying that these alone are not enough. If a man is going to "live up" he needs more resources. A poodle hardly needs Plato or a sow Socrates. But as human beings we need to get the whole picture. There can be no boundary line drawn with the notion that biological living is on one side and personal living on the other side; the two interact and interinfluence.

Some theorists regard the physical aspects as evil. Through the centuries various exponents of religions have discounted the physical nature of man and even the material stuff of the universe. The doctrine of asceticism held that man has to subdue the physical in order to be "saved." On the other side are those who frown at the "spiritual" and say it exists only in imagination. Thinking explorers have sought relationship rather than exclusion of one or the other. They have recognized the role of the physical body in the total program of living.

Existing or Living

A half century ago Stuart Chase posed this question: "Are you alive?" (*Reader's Digest*, September 1922). He wrote of what might be called the distinguishing line between "existing" and "living." He was honest enough to say that he himself did both. He reviewed a certain period of his life and made a lump estimate that he had been *living* about 40 percent of the time. He set forth such qualities as creativity, expansion of perception, and vital companionship as characterizing "living." He pictured himself as "existing" when he was doing things automatically. This applied to many social functions when he was "listening to dull people talk, discussing the weather." He considered himself "existing" when he lived with misunderstanding without endeavoring to achieve sound understanding.

Resources for "living" are not identical with resources for "existing," and the higher the level of living the more resources are required. We need to identify what constitutes these higher levels, then make connection with resources that will enable us to realize life on these levels.

Lower Levels Resources

Meet John Thompson. Think of him as "existing" very well in terms of getting along with others and with himself. He has a sturdy physique. He inherited and retained a body that has functioned exceptionally well as a biological machine. Where he lives, the air is clean and the soil is fertile. As he walks along his stride and posture would meet test requirements. These came to him "naturally." Sexually he adheres to the conventional code of his society; he has no hang-ups. Microbes have not made war on him. He responds to and makes use of resources in the way he was brought up to use them.

Yet John Thompson knows little about resources for "living up" and "living on." He goes to church when convenient and shakes hands warmly. Before and after meeting he talks with fellow farmers about things of common concern. He is at home talking about the condition of crops, his new tractor, the weather. He socializes well at church suppers and basket dinners. He relishes home-baked bread, fried chicken, and apple pie. He relaxes in a man-size chair with a foot rest watching what he likes on TV. But John Thompson has few available resources for the upper levels of living. He has never sought or cultivated these, although he has potential for such living. He has never gone over the resources that he uses in his own living. He has taken these for granted. And he has relied on others to take care of many social resources, locally and generally.

Presumptions About Spiritual Living

Meet David Stone. An "elder in the Melchisedec priesthood," he considers himself very "spiritual." He affirms that his major reading is in the Three Standard Books. In these he locates authority for what he does. He talks about "the fullness of the gospel." He gives the impression that he feels he has this fullness. His code for conduct is quite definitized. Most social pastimes are taboo. His conducting of meetings is standard. He uses the materials of services of his former years. The

Genesis story gives him his picture of the creation of the earth and of man. His calendar for human history points specifically to the ending of time and the coming of the millennium. He figures his tithing specifically; he would not underpay or overpay. David Stone is conscientious and consecrated—according to his own standards. He wants to be helpful to others in his prescribed way. And he tells the gospel to his limited world.

Yet David Stone puts up fences that shut off resources which would enrich his spirituality. He closes in revelation with fences of his own making. He has never become aware of the counsel that came to the Saints through Elbert A. Smith during World War I in which God advised, "I have many forces for good that you know not of." He concentrates on the evils of the times. He hews God to his own conceptions and "laws." This applies to the ministering of the Holy Spirit. God is expected to manifest himself in ways designated by this man. Well might God say to him, "I have resources that you know not of. Seek these resources; use them for 'abundant living.' "

Abundant Resources for Abundant Living

The phrase "abundant living" stands foremost for identifying life of high quality. Jesus told his disciples he came that they might have "more abundant" life (John 10). It is imperative that we "get with" this Christ and come to sense the kind of life he had in mind. There was nothing thin-blooded, or anemic, or retiring in his way of living. It was creative, courageous, dynamic, integrated, inclusive. It had eternal quality. He lived up, lived out, lived on. And he told his disciples that there were resources available to make this kind of living possible.

E. Stanley Jones, in the preface to his *Abundant Living,* wrote this counsel: "The business of life is to live well and adequately and abundantly. It is not enough to know *about* life, we must know *how* to live. We can pick life to pieces and explain its constituent parts and then fail miserably to put it together again in such a way that it becomes a coordinated, harmonious whole." On first reading we might think that Dr. Jones was presuming we had seen life as a whole before we started the dissecting. This is hardly what he meant. He was pointing out that abundant living calls for seeing the wholeness of things—seeing the total person in the total setting of life. The author's basic affirmation, pertinent to this study, is, "Life can never be abundant unless it has abundant resources" (page 1).

An organism cannot expend more in energy than it takes in from without. There have to be sources of energy on which the organism can draw. The process of restoration has to be continuous. This applies to human beings. A person has to be able to draw on resources if he is going to keep up to and, hopefully, rise above this level. He has to learn what these resources are and how he is going to relate to them. If there are none available or if he does not make contact with them he will sense defeat or experience decline. If he is able to make connection with resources for going on, he can experience restoration and renewal of life. If he does not find resources, he may experience personal incompleteness or insecurity or decline. Many experience what has been called "a sense of cosmic loneliness." Some cover up their sense of frustration or emptiness by hurrying to go nowhere or by getting busy in whatever is at hand.

"Abundant life calls for abundant resources." This means that the person has to be an explorer. He must explore what abundant living is, discover what resources are available for living abundantly, and determine how these resources are going to be used.

Discovering Other Resources

The story of humanity tells of man's discovering and utilizing resources that he had never known before—coal, electricity, atomic energy. The story of health tells of the discovery of many helps once unknown, such as insulin and penicillin. The story of psychology tells of the identification of "subconscious" forces and chemical influences hitherto unknown. In the area of plant life there have been findings such as pyrethrum, with its use for insecticidal and medicinal purposes, and the crossing of wheat and rye for a grain with high nutritional value and with increased sturdiness. And there has been some searching for spiritual reserves and resources.

Many of these newly discovered resources would have been hailed as impossible or the nonsensical notions of imaginative dreamers if the populace had heard of them before they came out with apparent advantages. The existence of oxygen and of man's breathing it would have sounded preposterous centuries ago. The story of mankind is crowded with ridicule or rejection of ideas that had to do with resources that man might tap.

This applies to spiritual things also. In honesty we need to admit that many unsound notions and practices have come to the fore. This does not give the right to exclude all suggestions and recommendations as foolish and fanciful. We have to distinguish between what is sound and what is unsound in this field of resources. We have to find out and identify what truly is in our universe and what exists only in wishful thinking, in hallucinatory dreaming, in retold tales. We need to distinguish between the valid and the invalid. We need to learn how to explore and experiment in the realm of spiritual happenings. We have had to do this in other fields. It is not for us to deny something simply because we do not understand it, because we have not yet experienced it. The great field of tapping spiritual resources is before us.

By Means or by Magic

Through the centuries many have sought to connect with resources through magic. This could be conducted by the person seeking "power" or through specialists in the field. The reliance on magic continues; in fact, there has been revived interest in it during recent years. In general the forces are thought of as falling into two groups—white magic and black magic. The latter forces are associated with demonic forces.

Three groups look to getting what they want through magic:

1. The superstitious. They do not consider that

things can be understood and predicted. They do not see that these resources can be tapped with any consistency. They think that things happen at the whim of whatever forces control things. So the way of getting wanted control is by doing what will induce favor of those who have control. Some believers in God feel this way. One man said quite frankly, "I try to make God feel good...for my own benefit."

2. The lazy. These people would rather do something that will get the Force or forces to come across rather than having to work to bring things to pass. They carry a general view resembling that of the superstitious.

3. The "quickers." They want things in a hurry. Rather than wait for cause-and-effect processes to take their course, these impatient ones seek instant results.

People who rely on magic do not look for understanding. They seek to manipulate by mood and shortcuts. Many see God as setting up borders which men are not to penetrate. Some think that spiritual resources are in God's province, and that men are not to pry into these matters. Knowledge is to be doled out on occasion, as God sees fit. This theory has been applied to flights to the moon during recent years. Explorers are looked upon as probing into God's own business. What is more, say these believers, man will not be able to see aright and interpret aright, for he is considered incapable of understanding top secrets in God's management of things. Some conscientious religionists take a somewhat magical attitude toward prayer. They believe man has to speak in a designated way in order to gain God's favor.

Increased Understanding

Some insist that in spiritual matters we have to understand and explain before we utilize spiritual resources. If we were to take this view in everyday life, we would soon be dead. We would not eat any food until we understood the processes of digestion and cell growth. We would not breathe until we could interpret the processes of respiration. In wise living we utilize resources while we keep on exploring and explaining. Many see the functional outcome of doing things while they do not understand the resources that makes things happen. These are of the mind that understanding will come as they live searchingly. Such was the man who said in the early days of electricity, "I don't know what it is, but I know that it works, and I know that it always works the same way." This man placed the resources of electricity above chance and magic. Although he could not explain it, he could say, "It works, and it works reliably."

All this applies to exploring in the field of the Holy Spirit. There is a wide range of views in considering the Holy Spirit as resource. This term "resource" bothers some, for it strikes them as being too "practical." Some consider the Holy Spirit as supernatural and thus beyond human understanding. On the other hand are those who insist that they will have nothing to do with this Spirit, unless they can describe and explain it. Some say that the Holy Spirit may be understandable, but human beings are not spiritually mature enough to perceive and interpret it rightly. Some say that the Holy Spirit is natural process which man is to seek to understand, and that only as he explores and experiments will he be able to utilize this "spiritual resource" safely and effectively. These consider that with increasing experiencing and maturing man will be able to utilize this Spirit more adequately, more fruitfully than today. Some with a lofty conception and a practical turn toward things advocate that as man grows in understanding of the Holy Spirit, he will understand many things he does not understand today and that the frontier will push out and he will see more and more in the "unknown" yet to be understood. Such a person will ever live where the now-understood and the not-yet-understood meet.

Theistic Affirmations About Resources

Theists believe in God. These believers hold to the belief that man needs resources for living and that God has an ample supply. There is enormous range in beliefs about what these resources are and how man is going to go about receiving them. At one pole are those who think of God as a cosmic Santa Claus who hands out favors to those who are "good little girls and boys." At another pole are those who think of God as the far-away Manager of the universe which is like a great scheduled machine that operates by rules and regulations. Beliefs range from working with God to waiting for God. Some view man as being of little importance and thoroughly dependent on God for everything. On the other side are those who believe that man is endowed by God to stand upon his feet, seek understanding, and work to bring things to pass with God.

God is visioned in many ways and on many levels. If we are to explore into these spiritual resources we must consider more than whether we believe in God. We have to be concerned with *how* we believe in God.

Our exploration about the ministering of the Holy Spirit involves inescapably the picture we have of God, of man, of the universe, and how these are brought together in Jesus Christ. We shall picture this on the level and in the setting where we are. We shall expect to keep growing and developing abilities and inclinations for continuing exploration and revelation. The study of getting with these spiritual resources will be lifelong, eternity-long. This can be a thrilling experiment.

The climactic statement of the theist is often that of Apostle Paul: "Our sufficiency is of God." Paul wrote this out of his own experience. And his experience kept expanding. In his farewell letter to his "gospel son" Timothy he wrote that while some persons had let him down God had ever been with him in an adequate way.

Present-tense living emerges out of past-tense happenings and moves on into future-tense experiences. The focus point is on the present, although this time point keeps moving on. The person has to have resources for living today. There has to be something, somebody to draw on, if life is to continue. *Homo sapiens* cannot postpone taking in oxygen until the next century or even until the next hour. He cannot wait until he gets the exact type of air he wants to breathe (but if he is foresighted he will see that the air is good). Some persons automatically breathe for themselves and leave the work of improving conditions to others. And this applies to spiritual resources. Many do little or nothing and draw on the resources of others. They have indirect appropriation. One day a man said to his God-believing friend, "You take care of this God stuff and maybe I can get a little benefit from you."

The person of growing vision will set forth clearly to himself the kind of life he wants to live. This will include the kind of persons with whom he will be consociating. And he will designate the resources he will need to realize this kind of life. Some of these resources will come to him through others. Some he will work for directly. And the Holy Spirit will be part of his reserve bank. He should have zest in his exploring, and the word should stand forth: "Abundant living calls for abundant resources."

Our Universe
Is a Bank
Of Resources

A bank differs from a depository or a museum or a mausoleum. A bank is in business. It is for continuing use of money—exchanging, loaning, financing. A depository is a safe storage place for monetary materials. Such is Fort Knox in the United States—federal depository for gold. A museum is an exhibition place where things are tagged and kept as they have been. A bank is a functioning institution in the ongoing world of business.

Our universe is a bank of resources, ever in process. Sometimes we speak of things that are "stored" in our planet, Earth. But everything stored here is ever in action. Our planet is no museum for keeping things as they have always been. Nothing in the universe that we know about "stays put." Sometimes the action is slow, sometimes rapid, but change is continual. Our universe has much for us to see, but nothing is placed on an exhibit counter or a museum wall or in a depository vault. Everything is in motion. And this cosmos is for us a bank of resources.

69

Many people want things to be "fixed" for now and always. This hope has been prominent in the outlook of many devout religionists. A man of middle age opined, "I would like to have lived in the Garden of Eden before man sinned. Then things would have stayed just as God made them." And another said, "It will be so wonderful when we get to heaven and things will stay perfect." A youth, weary of social uncertainty and confusion, commented, "I hope we get Zion built soon. Then things will keep going the right way...I mean established...they'll stay put." In the minds of these believers finality and purity go together in a finished perfection. For them change implies movement in an undesirable direction. A woman bothered by meal planning expressed her hope of heaven: there would be plenty of celestial ambrosia, so there would be no need for changing menus. She said, "In heaven food will be perfect, always the same." And a friend responded, "I would like to have a different dish at least once in a millennium." Many want to think of a universe fixed in goodness and heaven finished in stable perfection.

Fixed Perfection

The concept of perfection as a finalized happening has been and is quite prevalent. Whatever is perfect has been considered as eternally complete, beyond any practical or theoretical improvement. Many who want this fixedness read and quote Paul's comment to the congregation in Corinth. He was endeavoring to get his fellow saints to mature in their notions and practices of spiritual inspiration. They were stressing some dramatic manifestations out of right proportions. He wrote: "When that which is perfect shall come, that which is in part shall be done away" (I, 13:10). He was pleading for expanded vision and increased understanding. He was hoping for spiritual growth, not for spiritual fixedness.

Two men stood by a calm lake. One compared this peaceful body of water with the boisterous ocean of contemporary living. He said to his friend, "This is my dream of what life is to be as we get with God—not a ripple, not a strain, just peace." His friend said, "If this lake were as still as you think, it would be stagnant. There are springs at the other end continually bringing in fresh water. And when rain falls, water flows into the lake. There is also a small stream flowing out of this lake. Fish and other marine life are living in the water. This quiet lake is very much in action." The one man saw peace and perfection as ever in process; the other saw it in a situation of inaction. This contrast speaks the difference in views about spirituality—ever in process or finalized in quiescence.

This contrast is apparent in our thinking about the Holy Spirit. Our thinking about the Holy Spirit involves our thinking about the universe, and sometimes this gets pretty jumbled. Some believe that the Spirit brings peace, mainly to a still, calm world. For these perfection could not permit any change. Some think of the Spirit as promoting spiritual exhilaration inside the person and between persons without involving creative workings on the outside (God would take care of this). Others see a heavenly existence involving a universe ever in process, with man and God in cooperative living. These live by the affirmation in Doctrine and Covenants 32:3: "The power of my Spirit quickeneth all things." God is in action; the universe is in process; and man lives accordingly. The application is present-tense, and the "quickening" is continuing.

Resources

Originally "resource" carried the connotation "to rise again." A resource was thought of as something that would afford vitality. We can think of it as a force which enables us to "get up and get going." It is imperative that we see where we are going and how a resource will function in our getting there. A good resource for one activity can get in the way for another. A resource misunderstood or misused can be a liability. Any resource has to be seen in the light of its mission and utility. It takes up-and-coming persons to perceive and utilize resources. It takes a wise, panoramic view of life and of the universe for these resources to be seen in balance, and the user needs to see what life is all about.

To say that a thing is good is not enough; exploration must be made to ascertain what it is good for. Two men drove up to a filling station. One asked for gas, and the other asked where the drinking fountain was. With a sense of humor the second observed, "Let's not get mixed up and put the water in the gas tank and the gasoline in me." Used in the right way, both were necessary; used in the wrong way, they could result in disaster.

Genesis Directive

In the opening chapters of Genesis the story of creation is given as the Hebrews perceived it. The account is brief, with things seemingly happening almost instantaneously at the edict of God. We go to Genesis not to find out how creation took place but to get a few basic affirmations about what took place. In it we find the summary statement that God looked at what he had created and said, "It is good!" His pronouncement applied to the physical things of the universe. There was no line that placed material things on one side as evil and spiritual things on the other as good.

After man had been created, God gave him a directive. In essence he said, "This is for you. Take over." Here was to be a stewardship of management, of utilization (Fittingly, the place where man was to live was called a garden.) It is worth noting that God had sufficient confidence in man to warrant assigning him this stewardship.

Adam's world had the radius that his eyesight afforded. He had to find out what was in the garden and what he was to do with it. He had to discover what constituted living, especially living in God's design. Adam had no chemistry laboratory, no telescope for seeing the heavens, no microscope for looking at cells in a growing body, no thermometer for measuring temperatures, no cyclotron with magnetic involvements, and no library for research. He was a beginner in every respect, and he did some unfortunate blundering.

Today we are not in the Garden of Eden; we are in

the garden of exploration. We are still beginners in many fields, but we have more means, more machines. We have libraries and laboratories. We have come a long way, but we are still beginners. We must continue exploring to find resources and tap them for our benefit. We must discover more about this bank of ours, the universe. In our larger moments we hear God calling us to co-create with him so we can look at what we create and say, "This is good!"

Taboos

A taboo sign says, "Stay out of here!" Many taboos have no printed signs; they merely exist in our feelings. Through the centuries most of them have evolved out of views that it would be dangerous to enter some areas. This persists. The Greeks felt this way about Mt. Olympus; they said it belonged to the gods and man was to stay out. The Jews had this view toward the sacred rooms of the temple, and especially toward the Ark of the Covenant. There were notions that the human body was not to be invaded. This was God's province. Some denounced the work of William Harvey in exploring blood circulation. This was God's secret, and men were not to tamper with it. During recent years in one place in southeast Asia an incomer sought to help the natives procure a constant water supply with greater convenience. A spring some distance away was tapped with pipes for carrying water to where the people lived. On the day the project was completed the people gathered for a ceremony. The tap was turned, but no water appeared. Then it was discovered that priests of the region had gone secretly and pulled out the pipes. They were not going to suffer the curse of the gods who would be angry about this interference with the way the gods had planned to water the earth.

This turning away from exploration because of taboos has applied to much of the physical resources in the universe. It has applied, too, in other fields. Taboos about caring for corpses and conducting burials have been pretty powerful among many peoples. Thus the Parses of India never bury their dead, for this would contaminate the soil; corpses are placed on Towers of Silence, where the vultures dispose of them. Some conceptions and practices of religion are considered too sacred for human examination. Taboo is powerful. A conscientious man declared, "The Holy Ghost is to be experienced, never examined."

As God Has Provided

Many persons believe that God made things a certain way and nothing is to be changed. A few years ago several residents of a town in the central United States wanted to produce an "artificial lake" for adequate water supply. There was opposition from some staunch church members. Commented one elderly believer, "If God had wanted a lake there, he would have made it. He directed the Saints to gather here, with things as they were. I cannot and will not vote for constructing this lake. It would be interfering with God's pattern of things." Said another, "Let's use what God has provided, without interfering with the way he put things here." This notion of God's laying out things once and for all got in the way of managing resources for saving and storing water. And some took this stand in the matter of placing chemical ingredients in the soil.

Some have applied this way of thinking in the field of sex. Here is man's resource that can be managed this way or that way or let go without management. Some say that we need to understand and manage this sex resource. So here is a field for research, for freedom in expression. One says, "This is carnal and of devilish inclination. There is only one right use—for reproduction." And some consider that all that needs to be said about sex is in the regulations in the Bible, notably in the early chapters of the Old Testament. Others say that sex offers resource for reproduction but also for expressing closeness in person-with-person affection.

Unawareness in the Midst of Plenty

So often man has lived in the midst of this bank with rich resources and has not been aware of them. As indicated, primitive man lived around Niagara Falls, often in the dark and cold, without any awareness that one day this power would be harnessed and used for generating electricity. In ancient Greece men sent runners to carry their messages; they had no idea of waves that would carry sound. Atomic energy was all around but was unimagined and undiscovered. Yes, man has ever lived in the midst of the universe's resources, but until recently they remained unknown and untapped.

Now and then someone of exploring spirit would venture into the unknown. Benjamin Franklin with his kite found out about electricity. Galileo, exploring with a pendulum and falling bodies, opened the field of dynamics. He set forth his view about the earth in relation to the sun, making the sun of much greater size. When he was sixty-nine church authorities made him recant this view and "put the earth back in its place" as the immovable center of the universe. There is a story that as he rose from his knees after making his recantation, he muttered, *"Eppur si Muove"* ("It moves nevertheless"). With vision and courage he opened the resources through dynamics in physical energy. It is said that today we need Galileos in spiritual dynamics. Columbus risked a voyage across the Atlantic Ocean on the conviction that the earth was round.

These explorers opened fields for new resources against great odds. Sometimes they were called crackpots, sometimes dreamers, sometimes heretics. Many an onlooker, not understanding what they were working on, opined that their ideas did not make any real difference. Generally their pictures of the universe did not square with prevailing doctrines. Churchmen often had their thinking pretty well catalogued and closed in. They were inclined to think that their notions were God's notions. But many of these explorers opened up fields of thus-far unknown resources.

Discovering Spiritual Resources

So often we incline toward thinking of a "good universe" as permanent in its patterns. Small wonder that Koheleth said in Ecclesiastes, "The thing that has been is that which is going to be," concluding with,

"There is no new thing under the sun" (1:9). Koheleth was supposed to be complaining about monotony, but he was giving his view on the unchange of things. He was describing the universe as men in general thought about it. In such a world view the notion of continuing change was hardly wanted. In later years the faithful could sing, "Change and decay in all around I see." These thought of God as eternally static in perfection, with his universe finished off and his creation completed. There would be no worry about where things were going. Things had arrived.

God in Creative Action

Not all Hebrews bound God to past ways or tied him to things as they were. Isaiah, who began his prophetic work about 739 B.C., might have spent his time lamenting the condition of his nation. Assyria was threatening. The social and spiritual conditions of his people were not good. Yet he spoke constructively, affirming that Judah would not be annihilated. A "remnant" would survive to carry on. He counseled wisely; his country continued for a century and a half before its fall to Babylon. Isaiah spoke out boldly: "Sing unto the Lord a new song!" (42:10). In time he gave this message as God's affirmation: "I will do a new thing; now it shall spring forth!" (43:18).

Today we should not consider the bank of resources in our universe as a storehouse with supplies piled up and catalogued as in a museum—something to call for as we would items on the shelves of a store. Many do think this way. According to them God has a stock of goods on hand. If the devotee prays and promises aright, God's clerk will measure out and dispatch what the supplicant wants. Then the receiver can say that God hears and answers prayer. For some persons this applies to everything from the weather to health conditions.

In contrast, let us think of these resources provided by God as ever in process. God is creating as much today as ever. Were he to cease creating, he would become a past-tense God. The lines of continents are changing. A new island comes up out of the ocean. New timber grows. Some animals (such as the dinosaur) pass out of the picture. Resources are ever in process.

Human Effect on Resources

Modern man is to see his role in finding out about these resources and using them. He can do this to their benefit or harm (as he can do to himself). He can cultivate soil so that it erodes or he can preserve its productivity. He can send gases into the atmosphere and pollute it and dump garbage into the waters, or he can utilize these apparent nuisances for good.

What man should do to these materials has been the source of difference of opinions. In one tribal group the notion of controlled breeding of animals was not well received at first. Here was something that should be left to Mother Nature. When some of the first crossing of fruits and vegetables for new species was taking place, some objected. Species should be left as God started them.

And now scientists are exploring in the field of human reproduction and genetic processes. Rightfully do we ask, "What will the consequence be? Are they in accord with God's designs for man? Will we be having persons or biological specimens of Homo sapiens?" The social implications and moral involvements get pretty complex. And they are so important. Here it stands out definitely that we can affect many resources, including those in ourselves. It is high time for us to achieve clear insight into God's intent for these resources.

Contrasting Resources

We are coming to see how contrast and opposition function in the universe. We see this as holding together rather than as tearing apart. Long we have heard of centripetal force and centrifugal force. We think of this with respect to a body rotating around a center. The centrifugal force draws outward and the contripetal force draws inward. Rather than tearing the universe apart, this contrast enables it to continue. There are gravitational pulls that draw toward the heart of the planet and the galaxy pull that draws toward the outside. The existence of this tension enables celestial bodies to have predictable orbits. This is natural. This does not imply dualism or disintegration of our universe. It speaks dynamic and continuity.

Benjamin Franklin surprised many when he spoke of two kinds of electrical charge—*positive* and *negative*. The notion of opposite charges seemed to suggest the danger of a universe tearing itself apart. Then this functioning of opposites was recognized as a force for holding things together. This awareness of contrast came to the fore in exploration about the atom. The atom contains the neutron, which is electrically neutral; the proton, with a positive charge; and the electron, having a negative charge. These charges are viewed as equal. In the atom the continuous whirling around the central core goes on and on, with the tension making the atom hang together.

There appears to be this quality of contrast in the large stock of resources in the universe. This calls for consideration of contrast in resources that are not physical. We are stimulated to consider whether there could be personhood without contrast. If there is only one possibility for action, how can there be the decision-making which is requisite for maturing? Could there be personhood in a Garden of Innocence in which behavior is automatic? Resources in the universe seem to be designed for personhood development.

At the Service Window

"How much will the service charge be?" is a common inquiry at a bank window. The practical person guards against exorbitant rates of interest, unsound attachment of properties, and the like. Sometimes there has been an attitude against any charge for services. The term "usuary" came to be applied to high rates of interest. Hebrews in ancient times took a definite stand against usury. At that time they were primarily a pastoral and agricultural people. To them a loan was not a business transaction but an act of charity. Later the Jews were scattered through Western Europe and did not hold lands. Then they went into money lending with emphasis. Usury took on a different tone for them. Now in Western commercialism we expect a "service charge." We examine its terms and its expectations from the recipient and for the one who loans.

Often Christians have described religion as "thoroughly free." These believers have said much about "the grace of God." The big requirement designated has been that the person has to "ask of God in faith, believing." Then God would respond with salvation. Fervent songsters would sing, "Salvation is free, salvation is free! Jesus paid all, and there's no cost to me." An exaggerated expression of this is the testimony of an older man who said, "I've been saved thirty years and it hasn't cost me a dime."

There is another view which has no place for usury but requires getting with God in the managing of these resources. Here there is the relationship in which persons are to be "co-workers together with God" (I Corinthians 3:9). What one brings to God is not a service charge but a stewardship return on investment. Such service gifts are given to God (1) for the good of the giver, (2) for rapport of the giver with the "great Givee," and (3) for the good of the common enterprise of "God and Saints, Inc." This giving is essential in the development of abundant living. God insists that we give because we need to give for our sake. And there are stipulations about this giving. It is to be done with understanding. It is to be wholehearted—and whole-sighted. The gift is a vehicle for getting God's work on the way.

This huge bank of resources beckons us to explore. This includes both outer space and inner space. Albert Einstein is credited with saying, "Out yonder there was this huge world...which stands before us like a great riddle." He used the word "mysterious" to express his attitude. And always he expressed reverence and humility. He felt responsibility to interpret things aright, to advocate using aright the resources men would discover and tap. He was a genius, immeasurably great in his field of energy, of relationships, of movement in physical phenomena. He lifted all this above ordinary materialism. And the explorations have been continuing, especially in the field of atomic energy.

We need other Einsteins in other fields. We need Einsteinian insight into spiritual reality, into spiritual energy. This exploration would utilize what Dr. Einstein set forth. We might create a formula as he did and say that spiritual energy equals man in active relationship with God. We might put it something like this: $S.E. = M.G.$

Foremost in the list of resources to be discovered and understood and utilized is the Holy Spirit. This belongs in and is harmonious with our dynamic universe, so charged with motion and energy. We have come to sense something about the atom, unbelievably small and charged with power and movement. We shall do well to bring this searching intent into the field of spiritual resources and phenomena. We can be even more thrilled than we have been with the wonders of the atom. There is this difference: exploration into this field would be a personal experience. We need to see the spiritual energy in this bank of resources. We need to discover how this is available. We need to see what can happen in the utilization. The Spirit awaits.

And
There Is
Spiritual Reality

This consideration is foundationed on the basic that in our universe God provides spiritual resources that are are available to us as we have contact with him. He will grant us this spiritual dynamic as we line up with him. Without such requirement there would be chaos, not a cosmos. We have to accord with the ways of reality if we are going to utilize it. And this applies to spiritual reality. Here is the place for the functioning of the Holy Spirit.

Partial View

Through the centuries man has used the term "universe" with the view that there is oneness in everything, but seldom has he truly thought this way. In the Western Christian world there has been an inclination to act as if this universe were a dualism (as applies to the whole of things and to man), and God has often been thought of as conducting the universe in this two-part way. In initiating science studies man has inclined this way. First he asked questions that would be assigned to fields of astronomy and physics and related fields. For some time he did not deal with the biological body. Here was where dualism came to the fore. In man were the two opposing parts: material and spiritual. And this field was God's, for God was looked upon as giving man some special creation and destiny. Religion was placed outside the accepted territory for exploration and research. It was as if a sign had been erected warning, "Keep out!"

A Working Designation of Religion

In this exploration religion is going to mean man's relationship to the universe, personally conceived. This denotes a living, inclusive relationship (based on the assumption that there is some reality in the universe with whom man can relate personally). Here man is considered a person in a functional sense, and religion is seen as inspiring concern in what happens in man's personhood. It follows that, with such forces in the universe, man is living below his potential when he disregards this spiritual resource (either by deciding that there is nothing of this nature or by relating in ineffective ways). Both the sound and the unsound, both the stifled and the expanding procedures will pass under the title "religion."

This identification of religion as man's relating to the universe personally carries an inclusive application. Here is the posit that in the universe there is "Something personal," with whom man can relate in personal ways. This does not mean that the universe should not be designated as "spiritual." When man as person interacts with another person, the total body is involved. He expresses his personality through his body equipment, but there is something more than the physical in this expression. The universe can be thought of in this way—everything in it matters. But a more specific expression in the total universe can be designated as spiritual. Religion, then, deals with the whole, with emphasis on spiritual functioning.

Religion is man's personal relationship with the spiritual realities of the universe.

Semantic Clarification

Some words come to have such general connotation that we hardly know what they mean when we use them with one another. Often religion is this kind of word. It has come to denote ever so much—from fearing to fellowshiping, from adoring to acting with, from working to bring to pass to wanting by magic, from living abundantly here to waiting for glory hereafter. One youth commented that he could not say whether he wanted anything to do with religion, because it meant "everything from soup to nuts and I don't know what kind of soup and what kind of nuts."

The same applies to the term "God." Today when a thinking person is asked if he believes in God he will likely say, "What do you mean by God? I cannot answer what I believe about God until I find out what you have in mind. If you mean one thing, I shall say 'Yes.' If you mean something else, I shall say 'no.'" Here God has to be indicated in this conception of religion. He is the Great Somebody with whom man can relate personally in sound ways that square with

His kind of universe. And "spiritual" indicates the reality in which man can experience this relationship.

Views of Reality

Certain believers in God hold that there can be nothing evil. They say that God would not create a universe in which there would be evil. Mary Baker Eddy in *Science and Health* (published in 1875) affirms, "Evil has no reality...man is God's spiritual idea." In His order of things there is no sickness, no sin, no sorrow, no death. Such are "errors of mortal mind," and they have no reality except as man admits them. When he denies them, they cease to exist. This movement grew out of concern for human well-being here and now. In such a theory and program much of reality is denied existence.

Materialists affirm that there is no reality in the universe that responds to God. They consider man's creation an accident or a chance. Bertrand Russell wrote that henceforth man could build "the soul's habitation" only on "the firm foundation of unyielding despair." Robert Ingersoll, the eminent atheist of a century ago, said that when man spoke out of the universe "the only answer" would be the "echo of his mournful cry." H. L. Mencken wrote a half century ago his summary against hope "out there." He made these three statements: (1) "The cosmos is a gigantic fly-wheel making 10,000 revolutions a minute." (2) "Man is a sick fly taking a dizzy ride on it." (3) "Religion is the theory that the wheel was designed and set spinning to give him the ride" (H. L. Mencken, *Prejudices*, Third Series, page 132).

In fairness, I must note that not all these men surrendered to whatever might take place. Dr. Russell advocated and worked for a better world, contributing to the realization of good life for man. But he expected no "outside help."

This view of the universe is expressed forthrightly in the Charvakas or Lokayatas of India in their thoroughly materialistic school of thinking. They reacted against the denunciation of the material body by many Hindus. For them, only matter is real. Sense data are the only source of knowledge. An "abundant life" of the senses is the only good. Everything in a person ceases to exist when at death the body dissolves. There is nothing in the universe to respond to man. Man is on his own.

From Presumption to Understanding

Effective relationship has to be constructed on sound perceptions of the way things are. This applies to what a *person* is, what *personality* is. It also applies to reality. We ought to be concerned about reality because, as one man said, "We have to live with it." Then he added, "I want to know what makes up things and how they carry on; this gives me basis for getting on with." By and large today we are not concerned with big notions about "what everything is." We are more concerned about "what everything is doing." We see that we are related to things about us, including the universe. How we see this makes a significant difference.

The moon provides an illustration. Men used to think that the moon (called luna) sometimes exerted an unhealthy influence; those afflicted by it were called "lunatics." Later, noting physical effects on the earth, some observers concluded that the moon exerted an influence on tides. Interpretations ranged from magic to natural law. Recently we have explored the moon by traveling on it. We have reason to believe that it may have more and different influence than we have supposed. Some people see this going to the moon as invading God's own matters. Some see it as disproving heaven, since space travelers have gone beyond where heaven was supposed to be. Others are exploring fields of light, of "rays," of pulls and powers. They see the moon functioning in a universe of enormous span. And still others see the light, the life afforded through the Holy Spirit, expressed in these new discoveries.

Pervasive Spiritual Resource

Some think of the resources of the universe as a bank of supplies with compartments labeled "spiritual resources," "material resources," "intellectual resources," etc. Some who view praying and blessing in this light have specialized "saints" to preside over a field of living. Thus, the appropriate specialist would be approached if one were going to travel, plant a crop, raise cattle, compete in sports, or initiate a romantic association.

But spiritual resource is pervasive. The Holy Spirit is not to be visioned as a pep tonic or data dispensary. It pervades the universe, in diverse functioning. The Spirit always has been associated with light. Man becomes enlightened when he has relationship with this Spirit in an identifiable way. And this accords with modern conceptions of how light functions in the universe. In energy and light the factors called material and spiritual are not divisible. There is one process. In the inclusive sense all things may be considered as spiritual although expressed through material media. There is no antithesis between the two; both are emphases of total reality.

Resources for Personhood

Dr. A. N. Whitehead once spoke of "self" as "an emergent process arising in and through process." There is nothing static about the self, about personhood. The relationship with person-producing forces keeps going on, bringing changes, requiring continuing adjustment. This simple conclusion stands forth: One draws on some resources in the universe that enable him to become a person. I shall designate these resources as "spiritual." They are more than the forces that enable man to live as an animal; they enable him to have a self, to be a person.

An obvious counter would be, "This something is other persons." Certainly this is in the picture. Persons interact to produce personhood, and such interaction can go on and on, but this is hardly enough. There needs to be some reaching into the cosmos itself.

In this exploration the Holy Spirit is nominated as resource for producing personhood.

Need for Care and Humility

Religion is crowded with doctrines about how man can contact this Somebody in the universe. Too often there has been the tendency to identify and limit it in terms of patterns of thinking. This has happened in man's identification of light. There were notions about ether, waves, rays, and more, but in recent years light has been explained in larger ideas. Through the centuries Christians have been inclined to interpret the "spiritual" in confining ways.

One day a fervent believer said that he needed the Holy Spirit—right away. He did not consider the value of what he wanted in terms of God's ongoing program. He did not consider his own fitness to receive this Spirit. He did not think of his capacity to "contain" and "use" it. He was the center of his universe. He resolved to fast from three meals, keep praying, and make a financial offering. This would swing God over to granting what he wanted.

Further conversation disclosed that what this man wanted was the gift of prophecy so he would be able to stand in the congregation and say, "This is the word of God to you." He wanted the Saints to recognize him as a "truly spiritual man," thus elevating his status with his fellow members. What he needed was a prolonged study of what the resources of the universe—notably the spiritual resources—are for.

Being both humble and confident, we should say the way we identify the Holy Spirit is the best we have to date, that here is something so rich that our powers of identifying it are limited, and that we are going to work for greater experience and clearer interpretation as we live on. But we shall refrain from the view that we cannot reach out for this spiritual presence because we do not understand it completely. This would be like saying that we are not going to breathe until we understand the process of respiration, and that we are not going to eat until we can interpret the digestive process. There are those who say this kind of thing about spiritual matters. They overlook the truism that experiencing and interpreting go together, with supplementary influence.

Here we may well set forth a new beatitude: "Blessed is the man who reaches out to relate with the Holy Spirit, in wisdom, in love, for he shall grow in the understanding and the functioning of the Good Spirit in the living of persons."

Discounting Personhood

Some religionists discount the value of personhood. They consider human life burdensome and painful. For some the desirable goal is to lose identity as a person and merge into the ocean of reality. Life as a person is considered too harsh, too full of troubles, so they want to abandon personhood. In some Oriental religions this discontinuance of personal identity comes through getting rid of desire. Sometimes this fund of desiring is considered the force that draws man back into a reincarnate state. Desire keeps prolonging life. The hope is that man will be able to lose all desire and float at death into the great ocean in which personal identity is lost. This "ocean," although it might be thought of as having something of personal quality, could not mean much. Since a person is self-aware and self-managing; such an approach really amounts to eliminating personhood. There would be no place, no want for cosmic spirit that would further the quality of a person and contribute to his relating to others, to whatever there might be in the universe as person-producing.

Courage to Face Reality

In *Leave It to the Spirit* John Killinger sets forth the need for "courageous, perceptive persons" who dare to "alter the way we perceive reality." This involves the way we experience the world around us. Today we see that matter has never been so precise, so regular, so small as our forefathers believed. It is not as fixed, as static, as many supposed. We see it ever in motion, ever in process. We see it structured from microcosmic particles to gigantic solar bodies. A half century ago we thought of matter and energy as two aspects that would ever continue as such. According to the relativity theory, however, matter can be changed to energy and energy can be changed to matter. On December 21, 1941, scientists started a chain reaction that could keep itself going. On July 16, 1945, the experiment with an A-bomb was successful on the New Mexico desert. We have learned that the temperature at the center of the sun is nearly 40,000,000 degrees. We have developed the cosmotron for atomic research and learned how a particle can travel in one second a distance greater than from the earth to the moon. We are jarred and stimulated as we set forth to perceive this phase of reality.

We have to keep exploring for ongoing relationship. If a religionist were to say things in the spiritual realm as seemingly fantastic as scientists bring forth about atoms and cosmic rays and the enormous distance involved in their travels, he might be branded as having a wild imagination! This venturing of scientists came to the fore in the CETI (Communication with Extra-terrestrial Intelligence) conference held in Byrurakan, Armenia, in September 1971. Explorers wondered if there would be particles that travel faster than the speed of light for such communication. Earth's electromagnetic wavelengths would be too slow. This would involve the number of planets with temperatures and chemical conditions suitable for life. The scientists wondered if galactic energies would be available.

All this has to do with a vibrant, ever-in-process universe with phenomena of below microscopic size described in terms of billions of years and of distance in terms of light-years. Surely spiritual phenomena are to be included.

The Call to Total Reality

Dr. Leslie Dewart of Toronto, Ontario, said recently, "Religion is concerned with how man places himself in relation to reality." And I would add that this means total man in relation to total reality. As indicated our explorations in space, with atoms, and more have affected our approach to a program of living. Our discoveries and our conceptions make a difference. Every exploration brings out the picture of everything being in motion and ever in process. Such a universe has no place for a static God or a static celestial condition that marks the end of time and the end of creation. The God of such a universe must express in himself a synthesis of the total universe. There can be no dualism in which God keeps next to one part (the spiritual) and stays aloof from the other (the material). God has to be exempt from internal inconsistency which expresses the quality of evil.

We need to see these spiritual resources and utilize them for good living. Some resources we do not know about. Some things we see but do not see how to regard them as resources. Sometimes we glimpse what the naturalist meant when he said that a weed is a plant whose use we have not yet come to know. This can apply to ever so many things in the universe. Too often we regard spiritual resources as an uninformed man regarded some mineral resources: "First of all they aren't there, for there is no such thing. And what is more, if they were there I would not know what to do with them. They would get in the way." Often this has been said about the Holy Spirit. More and more we are seeing our good earth and our good heavens as resources for the good life. And we need increasingly to see the Good Spirit as essential reality, as indispensable resource for the good life.

We need also to see it as creative and exploratory in nature. Paul of Tarsus wrote to the Corinthians about the ministering of this Spirit. Since it was new to them, they were inclined to look for the dramatic and miraculous manifestations. He wrote of the Spirit, "He searches everything." Paul had pointed to the illimitable resourcefulness of God, of the teaching ministry of the Spirit. This speaks so directly, so functionally: "God has revealed the things of God through the Spirit; for the Spirit explores everything, even the depths of God himself" (I Corinthians 2:10).

This Is
God's
Natural Way

In this consideration we shall explore how the ministering of the Holy Spirit is "natural" in God's provision for man to develop personhood of eternal quality. This Holy Spirit inheres in God's cosmos; it is not added on to the order of things. God is seen as working through his Spirit in the past as well as now. He is not visioned as living in some distant celestial palace from which he issues orders and edicts. He is not seen as being on the outside and "intervening" now and then. Ministering through the Holy Spirit is his natural way.

Human Choice

Persons are designed to be self-managing. There are areas of living in which they have to make decisions or drift along. Some things they appear to do rather automatically—such as breathing. When a person gets neurotic about his breathing, counting the number of breaths per minute and feeling the movement of his diaphragm, an unhealthy state sets in. But there can be some self-managing in the respiratory process. Man can direct the nature of his breathing as to depth and outgo. He can plan to have the kind of atmosphere in which he is going to live. He can even go to the extreme of deciding that he is going to stop breathing by inhaling carbon monoxide.

Something like this occurs in the experience of the Holy Spirit. There is the pervasive presence of the Spirit in the universe affording life and light and love. This divine Spirit will function to hold things together without man's being conscious of it. But the personal inbreathing of this Spirit in personal nature calls for choosing on the part of man as person. God is not going to force his Spirit on anyone; a person has to reach out and respond and relate. He has to want this presence, and he has to qualify for it.

Supernaturalism

"Supernatural" has been used to denote things which are beyond nature. Terminology used in reference to the natural does not apply here...nor does any terminology. The "supernatural" is thought of as beyond our language resources. Believers in supernaturalism describe this as forces and happenings that are beyond what can be explained. In the Baltimore Catechism of the Roman Catholic Church "the Blessed Trinity" is referred to as "a supernatural mystery." Although persons cannot understand it, they are to accept it as "revealed by God." Here revelation does not entail understanding. In a former lesson distinction was made between natural and supernatural mysteries. "There are many *natural* mysteries such as electricity, radio, and magnetism. But since God revealed the knowledge of the Blessed Trinity to us, we call it a *supernatural mystery.*" V. Ferm's *Encyclopedia of Religion* makes this observation: "Supernaturalists hold that the nature of God is fundamentally different from that of the created world, so that any divine operation in the world must appear as something extraordinary."

This notion of supernaturalism sometimes complicates our designation of what is "revealed religion." Sometimes this has been designated as religion in which God reveals himself to man through ways which are supernatural. Thus revelation is placed outside the bounds of examination and evaluation. It is to be accepted on the witness, on the affirmation of those who are supposed to have spiritual discernment and authority. But others hold that revelation involves the natural powers of man and that man is capable of examining and interpreting what is set forth as revelation. And man has the responsibility to see what the revelation means, to say what it means, and to validate it in the laboratory of living.

Natural Law

There are two identifications of law: prescriptive and descriptive. The former sets forth what a person has to do. If he does not adhere, there will be prescribed penalties. This applies to civil law. A maximum speed for travel is set, and the person who goes faster may expect to be penalized. Much of the lawgiving in the Old Testament was prescriptive. For instance, a woman caught in adultery was brought before the people and stoned. And when a person did something against God, there were specific means of redemption for getting rid of the guilt. Youngsters pick up this idea from their elders. Some boys coasting down a wide hill on the snow passed an edict that anyone who got on the wrong side would have to stand aside during the next takeoff down the hill. Prescriptive laws are passed and published; the penalties are announced.

Descriptive laws express what happens. Observers note that in natural phenomena certain things happen under certain conditions. They are not decreed; they are discovered. Science makes the basic presumption that nature is more than happenstance; it is orderly and uniform and predictable. Men watch to see how nature behaves, and when something happens time after time with the same outcome, this is stated descriptively as natural law. For example, warmer air rises . . . water seeks the lower level.

Sometimes we have to reconsider what we have stated as a natural law. We do not denounce those who stated the law; we commend them for what they did and then bring in new data. Isaac Newton at the beginning of the eighteenth century formulated the law of gravitation which has to do with the pull on objects toward the center of the earth. Scientists built their work on the conviction of the uniformity of nature, but today there is questioning of this postulate. Nature is viewed as being in a state of flux. Things may not be as uniform as once presumed.

Descriptive laws are not "passed" or imposed. There

are those who think of God's creating the universe and then setting forth some laws for its operation. These would be prescriptive laws. Rather does natural law keep operating in the ongoing creating. Such law would describe the creative process.

Celestial Law

The term "celestial law" has come into fairly general usage. On first thought this might seem to refer to upper-level phenomena (supernatural). Not so. It refers to the descriptive indications of happenings in what might be called the upper strata of our human experience. We can say that celestial law indicates how God operates on higher levels, recognizing that there *are* levels of experience. Celestial living designates a way of life that most nearly accords with God's nature and purpose. This living includes the wholeness of things in fullness of relationship. The person relates with God and other persons. He sees with God in eternal perspective, in universal proportions. He is capable of perceiving natural laws where others do not see the phenomena and would not experience the happenings.

Celestial law describes the operation of God on this higher level, in this inclusive relationship. Celestial laws are more than edicts, more than commandments. They are descriptions about the way God's universe works in purpose, in process. They apply to all reality. Insight into these natural laws enables us to line up and live on with God. This is a matter of capacity and relationship. What a thrill to come up to celestial level, perceive natural celestial law, and live celestial life.

Identification of Natural

The word "natural" carries different meanings and moods. Especially is this so in the term "natural man." Paul was very intent when he wrote to the Corinthians to make sharp distinction between the "spiritual" man and the man who was not. He wanted the saints of Corinth to be concerned with major matters. They were inclined to squabble about things of less consequence. He emphasized the ministry of the Holy Spirit: "We have received...the Spirit which is of God, that we might understand the gifts so freely given us by God" (I Corinthians 2:12). In the King James version this comment follows: "The natural man receiveth not the things of the Spirit of God: for they are foolishness to him." The Revised Standard Version reads, "The unspiritual man does not receive the gifts of the Spirit of God, because they are foolish to him and he does not understand them." This helps us to see what Paul was endeavoring to say.

This phrasing comes out in the Book of Mormon. Good King Benjamin in his farewell address called his people to spiritual living: "For the natural man is an enemy to God, and has been, from the fall of Adam, and will be, forever and ever" (Mosiah 1:119). He spoke the same as Paul, with the word "natural" connotating "unspiritual." In the next sentence he speaks of yielding to "the enticings of the Holy Spirit" and of putting off "the natural man" and becoming "a saint, through the atonement of Christ." Here again this might read, "The unspiritual man is an enemy to God."

Alma, prophet in the Book of Mormon, came up

with this word "natural" meaning "unspiritual." He advised, "All men that are in a state of nature, or I would say in a carnal state, are in the gall of bitterness, and in the bonds of iniquity. They are without God in the world, and have gone contrary to the nature of God. Therefore they are in a state contrary to the nature of happiness" (Alma 19:75). Here Alma was saying that God intends us to live lives of qualitative happiness; when we get away from him, we lose the way to happy living.

The Original Nature of Man

God did not design a wicked, unresponsive man bent on hellish living. He designed a man to live up and to live on. He intended this man to be a person—with potential for choosing, with opportunity to make choices, with freedom to take the consequences of his choosing. Choice without consequence for choosing is not full freedom. God never compelled man or reduced him to abject fear. He wanted a man who would choose of his own volition to go along with divine will and be happy in doing so. This is the original—the natural—man.

Christian theology has made much of the fall. According to some doctrines man was so fallen, so depraved, that he was incapable of making a choice for the right. He was seen as helpless, as incapable of doing good, and God could come in when man was submissive, subservient. So often this picture of fallen man was taken as portraying "natural man." A misnomer!

After Alma spoke of man "in a state of nature" as

"contrary to the nature of God," he went on to speak of "restoration." This meant taking a thing of a natural state and restoring it to the natural way of living. When man got away from God and lived in an "unspiritual" condition, restoration meant restoring him to his original condition in which God intended him to live. The true natural condition of humanity is this lining up with God so that man lives the life of happiness. Alma affirmed, "Wickedness never was happiness" (19:74). God is ever calling man, ever wanting him to live restoringly in his God-designed natural state.

God, Orderly or Otherwise

Norsemen thought of their gods as acting on the spur of the moment. For instance, if Thor was agitated, he might throw out a thunderbolt, and devotees would do something to try to make him feel better. Some Christians see this quality in their picture of God. They feel they need to get God in favorable disposition toward them so he will be more likely to grant what they are asking for. A gift might help out. And some think of God's deciding and doing right at the instant. They think that he directs through the Holy Spirit in instantaneous expression. One elder said, "I always preach at the direction of the Spirit." When asked how the Spirit directed him, his reply was simple: "Before I get up to preach, I pray that God will direct me. I open the Bible and place my finger on a page. Whatever passage it touches is my text."

Others see God as long in purpose and orderly in procedure. His ways are reliable, predictable. These persons sense the necessity to try to perceive how God works so they can line up with him. Most believe that while God plans with this larger, longtime method of operation, he "comes through" in an emergency. Such persons note how some experience, probably dramatic and intense, which appears to happen all at once has a background that has been shaping up for a long time. Thus the Restoration happenings of 1820-1830 in western New York State had three or four centuries of foundation. There was the discovery of America and all that led to it. There was the Reformation with its complex background. There was the rise of parliamentary government with toleration of religions. All of these were part of God's program. In this type of thinking God is soon working in cause-and-effect procedure with things happening in sequence.

This conception of God entails "natural law," which means that God's ways, in process, in procedure, in employment of persons are describable. And this applies to spiritual reality.

The Long Way of Creating

God is ever creating. Were he to cease creating he would become a has-been. Many people think of God as having completed creation when he "finished" getting the earth in shape. Some used to designate this as Friday evening 4004 B.C. According to them the time span of creation was brief. Each thing was made all at once at the decree of God. It was as if God snapped his fingers and the earth or the moon or a cow came to be. To simplify matters (or to complicate them) there was the notion that God created everything out of nothing, *ex nihilo*. According to this theory there was nothing to describe in the creation process. No natural laws operated. God just gave the order and the thing appeared before him.

Today we are aware that there is no finalized universe, no finished Earth. Shorelines of our continents are shifting. Temperatures are not as they were a few million years ago. New islands come out of the ocean. Coral reefs continue growing. Some animals become extinct. And our sun with its millions and millions of years behind it is changing as it pours out its energy, with a small portion of it coming to our planet. Physical creation is still going on. And the processes of creation are describable, the processes that God has always used. The descriptive statements about these are called *natural laws*. And all this ongoing creation involves the functioning of the Holy Spirit.

God's Relationships with Persons

Some who see God proceeding in physical phenomena in predictable ways, with laws describing, turn aside when they come to personal phenomena. They consider man to be unpredictable as to ways in which he is going to respond to life situations. Furthermore they say that such natural laws would hem God in. If so, it would be God, not they who would do the hemming in. But these laws are to be seen as affording order and effectiveness rather than limitations. I admit that in the main man's reaction cannot be predicted because not enough is known about the factors involved. These factors may go back a long way, out a large way, and in a complicated way. God has the data for perception of persons.

Developments in studies of personality and inter-action of persons have come fairly recently. These have been related to biological studies, which have both helped and complicated the situation. Some-times, in this new era, conclusions which have been set forth as natural laws ought to have been regarded as only temporary statements made on the way. Thus some of Freud's comments about the drives that prompt and control men are now seen as partial and overconclusive. (This does not lessen the high regard for this pioneer in human behavior, but studies of these social sciences are just getting under way. There must be a blend of courage and humility.)

God relates to persons understandingly and with eternal perspective. He is concerned with the whole person. He takes a long time to develop a man, to get him ready for consequential endeavor. He works with a sense of cause and effect. His method can be observed.

A noteworthy case is presented in the first books of the Old Testament—the story of Moses' life. This reveals how God would see a man as he is, as this man sees himself, and as God intends him to become. God did ever so much laboratory work with Moses. There was no right-at-this-moment transformation. God moved from situation to situation. He took things as they were, where they were, and worked them through to effect happenings. Moses was a main character in these. Events related as turning points came out of pasts that were very complex. Such was the burning bush at Midian, the Passover in Egypt, and the crossing at the Red Sea.

God is the Social Scientist who works with persons in alignment with natural laws in human relations. He is the Father with close association as he uses these inherent laws. The Holy Spirit ministers.

Descriptive Laws with the Holy Spirit

Persons of honest insight do not say that they understand all the workings of the Holy Spirit. They do say that they understand better as they have more and more experience with the Holy Spirit, as they explore more and more in this field of spiritual reality. These persons take the Holy Spirit out of the realm of the supernatural and place it in the world of the natural.

It is evident that our conceptions will be partial and our experience limited, but description is possible. The pull of the yet-to-be-explored draws us on. If we were able to exhaust the field, if we were able to explain everything, the Holy Spirit would be too small to elicit our interest and exploration throughout our life-span...and on.

Here are some fields for us to explore that we may understand the functioning of the Holy Spirit and experience it more soundly. Such exploration can enable description in terms of natural law.

1. The nature of personhood that we say is to achieve "eternal quality"—the kind of personhood we are setting out to develop. (This involves identifying how the ministering of the Holy Spirit can function naturally with persons.)

2. The functioning of personhood in forms beyond our present human notions of what personhood is, the functioning of personal expression independent of the human body. (This would have bearing on the perception of the Holy Spirit as personal, with larger, freer functioning.)

3. The continuing creative process in our universe, with foundation for perceiving the integrating, creating role of the Holy Spirit.

4. The range in the capacities, the interests and concerns, the responses, the initiatives of persons, bringing out the requisite for diversity in methods, in message in the levels of spiritual ministries to men. (This carries implications for the inclusive functioning of the Holy Spirit, and for diversity in this functioning.)

5. Consideration of the biblical teachings about the Holy Spirit in an age prior to ideas of natural law, scientific research, and the conception of personhood—interpretation of such matters as "fruits" and "gifts" of the Holy Spirit in thought patterns of the present time.

6. Studies in language—verbal, sensory, and extra-sensory; the role of language in communication through the Holy Spirit, and the conditioning of this ministry of the Holy Spirit by our language potentials.

7. Education of church members in wholesome exploration of the Holy Spirit, in theory, in practice, with balance of experience and interpretation; study in the meaning of, the implications of setting forth expression of the Holy Spirit as "natural" as describable in terms of natural law.

108

An Open Field for Exploring

Traditionally miracles have been identified as unusual happenings beyond the borders of natural law, at the intervention of God. The discard of supernaturalism might seem to indicate the rejection of miracle. Not so. Some do reject it. Others redefine it. Let miracle be considered as a happening beyond the natural law known to date but within the range of natural law. The causal factors describing it are yet unknown. This means that there is not yet the experience, resources, or ability for interpreting it.

In a world where persons think and explore, the line between the understood and the not-yet-understood is always moving. In former times men not only said things were not understood; they designated some things as not understandable. Once lightning and thunder were placed in the realm of the supernatural; they were sent by gods. Man was not supposed to understand such wild happenings. Then came the explanation of lightning and other phenomena in the atmosphere.

There are fields long heard of and taken for granted that have never been explored soundly. Such is the Holy Spirit. Devotees have assigned it to the realm of the supernatural. Urgent religious speculators push it toward the spiritual supersonic. Cynics think of it as self-stimulation. The Holy Spirit needs to be studied as something natural, something inherent in God's universe. The natural man needs this natural spiritual resource.

SECTION B

Background
In Our
Christian Religion

In this section we shall reconstruct and relive the happenings of the first decades of early Christianity. We shall see Jesus and his Twelve as living men. We shall sense the spiritual impact that he had on these men and others. We shall search the ways he taught them so they would anticipate and be ready for the experiencing of the "other Comforter," the Holy Spirit. This section is foundationed on the conviction that what happened in the disciples' lives while Jesus was with them was to continue in the ministering of the Holy Spirit after he left them. We appreciate how they had to mature in their expectations, in their experiences with the Holy Spirit. We see under what conditions this Spirit was vital in ministry and in what conditions this vitality weakened. It is imperative that we see soundly, functionally the happenings during this often-called period of true "spiritual empowerment." We note factors in endowment and factors in decline.

Jesus
Drew On
Extra Resources

We look at Jesus of Nazareth and ask, "How did he keep going?" A modern man, busy with his work, civic affairs, and church life, asked this question. He had been reading in Luke of Jesus' years of ministry when he was living with and giving to others. This man added, "He did not have any pep pills or tonics." After further reflection he summarized his conclusion that this Jesus must have been drawing on "something that kept putting power into him." Reverently he added, "This must be why we call him Christ."

Jesus of Nazareth stands out as the man who drew on extra resources so he would keep having extra revitalization. His work was demanding. His association with others kept taking energy out of him. Sometimes the crowd or his friends would seek to draw him from his course. Frequently his enemies charged him with being in league with the devil. At times when he should have been receiving support from his disciples to help keep up his morale they could not grasp what he was trying to do. Occasionally they would set forth their own self-centered hopes. He came face-to-face with law-bound Jewish priests and military-minded Romans. He was with the average run of his own countrymen who wanted food provisions, physical healings, and deliverance from Rome—with some drama thrown in. These people kept wanting something from him, but Jesus never said, "Wait, I'm tired now." He never told people to go away, that they were not worth his time. He did not refer them to counselors of less caliber. Nor did he tell them to wait until they got to heaven. Always he was available, responsive, giving.

This Jesus drew on extra spiritual resources.

The Twelve-Year-Old in the Temple

The first picture we get of Jesus was when he was in the Temple at the age of twelve (about Bar Mitzvah age). Here he had firsthand contact with Jewish orthodoxy. The picture has been quite prevalent that Jesus was "telling off" his elders, but Luke's account has this significant comment: "He was listening to them and asking them questions" (2:46). The preceding statement is an abbreviated account of what had been happening in his life prior to this: "The child grew up and became strong and full of wisdom. And God's blessing was upon him." He must have been developing a wholesome curiosity, a concern about many things, and a wholesome set toward life. With this background, he turned inquiringly to the doctors of Jewish Scriptures.

Jesus must have had a healthy homelife. He is

described as working with his father Joseph in carpentering. Obviously he was allowed a measure of independence by his parents (when they left Jerusalem, they did not discover that he was not with them for a while). He was not trying to get attention or being a smart aleck. He was seeking information. Luke wrote, "All who heard him were astonished at his understanding and his answers." When his parents chided him for not being with them, he responded with a sense of mission, "Do you not know that I must be about my Father's business?" Then he returned to Nazareth...and kept on growing.

In this temple incident factors were expressed that said much about this boy's life. (1) He was lined up with God in God's business. He had something to live for. (2) He was inquiring about major matters, not just arguing about disputable points. (3) He was gaining confidence, not just whistling in the dark. (4) He was exploring beyond the patterns of his family, of his synagogue, of his fellowmen; he was adventuring with God.

The Test

Over the Jordan River came this salutation to Jesus, "You are my beloved Son!" This occurred when he was thirty years old—the conventional age for a Jew to take his place as a full-stature man. After his baptism "Jesus returned from the Jordan, full of the Holy Spirit." This Spirit was needed for exacting life situations which followed. What happened in "the temptation" gets right at choice-making in everyday living. Three critical decisions are presented in the account. These get at the kinds of life situations most of us encounter.

Crisis I. Jesus was hungry. (Crises often come at the point of our hungers, of our drives.) First, there was the disturbing "if." ("If's" figure prominently in our either-or situations.) "If you really are the Son of God," the tempter said, "command these stones to become bread." Here was the invitation to use available powers for personal gratification. But Jesus refused to misuse his resources.

Crisis II. First there was a survey of lands and peoples—then another if. "If you will worship me, all this will be yours." Here was bargain driving with low motivation. Straightforwardly Jesus rejected the offer. Genuine mission gifts have no strings attached.

Crisis III. This was an invitation to do some dramatic parading. Jesus was pictured as being on the highest ledge of the Temple. What a pretentious way to exhibit his divinity! The people would have gazed in wonder if the proposal had been carried out. Again came the if. "If you really are the Son of God . . ." Then the tempter quoted scripture: "He shall give his angels charge over you." Devils are pictured as being good scripture quoters and impish interpreters. On the whole, mature scripture students do not indulge in much quoting. They employ scriptures to help them see their situation and to get insight for meeting it. Jesus had no idea of drawing attention to his Messiahship by putting on a circus act. He used his resources to counteract the driving suggestions of his tempter. The Phillips translation contains this closing comment: "When the devil had exhausted every

116

temptation, he withdrew until his next opportunity."

Jesus did not compromise; he did not put off; he did not leave the deciding to someone else. This continuity line follows the account of the temptations: "Jesus returned to Galilee in the power of the Spirit" (Luke 4:14). The resource of the Holy Spirit had ministered during his time of need.

Unrecognized Food

While going to Galilee by way of Samaria Jesus met a woman at Jacob's well who had come for water. He was alone, for his disciples had gone into the city to buy food. Jesus did the unusual: he requested this Samaritan woman to give him a drink. She was surprised that a Jew would ask this of a Samaritan. Then Jesus added to her amazement by telling her about her life, which had been pretty muddled. But he followed this by offering her hope—by telling her of "the water of life." He exercised his penetrating and describing powers of discernment. The woman sensed his rare prophetic gift.

When the disciples returned their first request was simple: "Master, eat." Just then Jesus did not take any of the food they had brought, and they did not understand. They asked, "Has anyone brought you anything to eat?" Jesus replied, "I have food to eat, of which you do not know. My food is to do what he who sent me wants me to do." He gave this terse explanation: "To carry on his work" (John 4:34). Jesus wanted his men to sense the relationship between spiritual nutrition and spiritual exercise. This "extra food" does not come by sitting in a café, waiting for an angel to bring a plateful of celestial goodies. Nor does it come by "telephoning" prayers of requests for heavenly delicacies. It comes when a person gets busy with God and absorbs spiritual nutriment.

This incident in Samaria gets at some basics about Jesus' ministering and experiencing endowment for this ministry. (1) *The utilization of "extra" resources and the availability of these resources for ministering to others.* He expected that strength and vigor would come to him when they were merited. He would have run down had he not received resources for renewal. It is expedient to discover how far he went in this direction. Jesus took care of his body. (2) *The ever continuing hopefulness of Jesus Christ with respect to a given person.* He did not look at generalities. He got next to the person. His own resources provided means for exercising this persisting hope. (3) *The awareness of needed ministering in the immediate now.* Ever around him were persons such as this woman of Samaria, who needed spiritual guidance and encouragement—the spiritual dynamic that would radiate from his presence. That day he told his disciples that where they were that very day the field was "white unto harvest." Jesus demonstrated in his own living that spiritual sustenance is inseparably associated with spiritual exercise, expressed in reaching to others.

It was going to take these disciples quite a long time to discover what Jesus meant by the food that they did not know about, the food on which he relied. They had to learn that Jesus never discounted wholesome material food. Often would he eat with them. He even provided a fish breakfast for his eleven apostles just before he left them permanently (John 21:9).

In another fellowship circle with these men he confirmed and nourished them with the "extra food." They were inside locked doors because of their fear of the Jews. Symbolizing life-giving breath, so meaningful in their world, he breathed upon them and said, "Receive the Holy Spirit" (John 20:22). Then he commissioned them to go out and share the good news with others. This ministering would entitle them to extra spiritual nourishment. So compelling was this call and commission that John wanted to continue living and ministering.

On Mount Transfiguration

Jesus provided in his program of living for increasing his fitness and fortitude. He advised his disciples to do this also. Once after several busy days with people he said to them, "Come along to some quiet place and rest awhile" (Mark 6:31). They needed this for fellowship, for renewal, for perspective. He did this for himself, too. When it was time to call the twelve apostles, he "went into a mountain to pray" (Luke 6:12). This was an all-night communion.

Jesus was selective when he chose men to go with him on the more requiring projects. This was not a matter of favoritism. He chose for fitness for spiritual consocation. He would be able to do some things with some persons that he would not be able to do with others. The diagram of Jesus' associations would not be one of separate circles with some labeled "My Favorites." It would show concentric circles, with an inner core group. As Jesus moved toward the climax of his life he would arrange to have time with those men closest to him in spiritual fellowship. This time he took Peter, James, and John with him to a "high mountain apart" (Matthew 17:1). Here "his face shone like the sun and his clothes were white as light." Three resource expressions came to Jesus. These were needed to equip him to face the tremendous trial ahead: (1) divine luminance, (2) the support of ancient-time worthies, Moses and Elijah, and (3) the confirming salutation, "This is my'beloved Son: hear him!" Here he absorbed resources for coming days.

These happenings on the mountain made tremendous impact on the three men. A first reaction, voiced by Peter, was, "Let us build here three tabernacles!" (A criterion of sound spiritual experience is the desire to build.) Another reaction was fear combined with a sense of unworthiness. Confidence came when Jesus said, "Arise and do not be afraid." Healthy spirituality breeds confidence in the rightful outcome of things and at-homeness in the presence of God. Another basic was revealed in the salutation, "This is my beloved Son: hear him!" This high experience centered in communion with the living, caring Christ. This was more than a dogma or symbol about Christ. Here was Christ in person. He was with them.

Jesus implied that this experience was firsthand resource for what they were to be doing. They were not to stay on the mount; they were to go to the valley and minister to the people who needed the radiant influence they now could bring. They were not, however, to tell others about this experience until the time was right. They were not to advertise what had happened. Jesus was warning against publicity testifying. He was teaching that such impelling experiences are to be utilized for personal quickening rather than headlines. This was to be for resource rather than for report.

Alone, Without Resources

The closing scenes of the Crucifixion contributed much to the inclusive picture of the endowed Christ. Here was the portrayal of the tragic desolation and despair of a man bereft of every resource, completely alone. Here was the contrast between the Christ endowed by the Spirit of God and the man Jesus.

Here were soldiers, priests, a few uncertain believers, common folk who were not sure of what was happening, the curious who did not want to miss anything, the cynics. The taunt of "if" was in the air: "If he is the king of Israel, let him come down from the cross." This was followed by yet other taunts, "He saved others, but he cannot save himself.". . . "He said, I am the Son of God." Soldiers gambled for his clothes. Over his head was the inscription in Hebrew and Latin, "This Is Jesus, the King of the Jews," placed there in mockery. Mark tells pointedly what had happened with his disciples after the arrest in Gethsemane. "They all forsook him and fled" (14:50). His mother stood by the cross, helpless (John 19:25). One of the two thieves railed in derision. It was fitting that there was darkness over all the land (Matthew 27:45).

Out of this depth of agony came the lament of Jesus,

probably from Psalm 22, "My God, my God, why hast thou forsaken me?" (The next line of this Psalm might well have been added, "Why art thou so far from helping me?") This was neither a rejection of his Father nor a cry of loss of faith. It was a cry from the depths of his soul, a cry of loneliness. Jesus demonstrated what happens when a person is completely separated from divine resources.

Yet in those closing moments Jesus radiated his true self. When the rabble had quieted, when the disciples were saying nothing, when the priests were satisfied with what had happened, when the soldiers were doing their routine duty, a thief at his side spoke up: "Remember me when you come into your kingdom." When his enemies had done their worst and it looked as if everything he had stood for had collapsed, a dying thief saluted him as King.

His Continuing Personhood

The followers of Jesus did not exhibit much belief in resurrection. When he ceased breathing on the cross, to them his career was ended. The reaction of Simon Peter might be taken as representative reaction: "I go a fishing" (John 21:3). Some of his friends went with him. When Jesus appeared to them one morning after a catchless night they did not recognize him. He couldn't be there: they had buried him! Then John recognized him. Peter's reaction was typically impulsive. He had been fishing without clothes. Hastily he slipped on his fisherman's garb and plunged into the sea (John 21:7). The men were still more bewildered when they discovered that Jesus had prepared breakfast for them. There, in a circle on the seashore, they caught the impact of the continuing Jesus—his ongoing personhood, not just his body. Jesus brought extra help to these fishermen apostles that day, and they brought in a mammoth draught of fishes. His foremost concern was that they have what would be required to become "fishers of men."

Without Demonstrative Show

After the resurrection Jesus never showed himself to Pilate, Herod, any priests or officials, or those who scoffed and railed at him on the cross. If he had put on a vindictive demonstration, what an event this would have been! What misunderstandings would have occurred! Donn Byrne in his novel *Messer Marco Polo* sets forth a fitting picture. Marco Polo was wanting the lovely Golden Bells, daughter of Kubla Khan, the mighty ruler of China. One day Marco Polo stood before the Emperor on his high throne telling about Jesus. The auditors were impressed with stories of healings and other manifestations of power, but they were troubled with the account of Jesus' death. When the narrator said, "On the third day he rose from the dead," a great shout arose. Kubla Khan stood up and cried out, "Then he showed himself to Pilate, in all his majesty and power, and. . ." "No," said Marco Polo. "Then he showed himself to the thousands who had seen him die?" "No," said Marco Polo. The Emperor frowned. "Then to whom did he show himself?" And Polo answered, "To a few of his friends and followers." No more was said.

Jesus used his extra spiritual empowerment in

companionship with those who would catch the true spiritual dynamic that was in him. This would enable them to express redeeming, renewing power to others, and they would be able to say that they knew the real Christ Jesus.

In Personal Consociation

Jesus never went back to those who had condemned him and said, "I told you so." He showed himself to those who would catch the meaning of his resurrection and said, "I send you forth." He told them that they would have the necessary empowerment for their work. Clayton Williams wrote in *The Dark Road to Triumph:* "The resurrection is not primarily to tell how long life lasts but to reveal what lasting life is like" (pages 106-107). This resource has to be lived with rather than looked at. Dr. Williams added that what happened "was not to convince skeptics but to empower saints" (page 107). Jesus' ongoing life was to be resource rather than exhibit. This resource was to function in consociation rather than in conjecture or computation. He promised continuing resource in being with him—the living, triumphant, dynamic Christ. Ever he tells his disciples, "Lo, I am with you always" (Matthew 28:20).

Jesus Conducted
A Laboratory School
In Personal Living

"They went to school with the Christ; they lived with the Great Teacher." So commented a modern man about the early Christians, especially the apostles. Theirs was a laboratory in living together with God. His spiritual dynamic was expressed vitally through their teacher, Jesus. Theory and practice were combined in their on-the-job training. Their school was in the ongoing stream of life on earth. Their teacher expressed the kind of living that he set out to develop in his men. He was their living textbook. He radiated the spiritual power his men needed in order to find God, to find themselves, to find others, to find the Way. Here was (and is) the first-class school of all time.

There were twelve men in this school. It was not a large university with an enrollment of thousands, but it was a university in the true sense that it had to do with the universe in universalizing ways. Jesus never put up bulletins in order to draw in crowds. He wanted a number suited to carrying on a laboratory school. This was a group chosen to do a job together.

These men were to radiate out in personal chain reaction. In a company of this size every member of the school could interact with the others, getting to know each as a person. There was to be no one sitting on the sidelines or watching from the bench. Every man was to be on the playing field. And their coach, Christ Jesus, would be in the midst of the game of life with them. He would involve them in the relatedness required on the gospel team.

If the number had been too large, the men would have been deprived of the fraternity needed for common endeavor. If the number had been as small as three or four, they might have developed a narrow, provincial outlook—could have developed a limited view of human nature and human reactions. As it was, Jesus had to keep working with his apostles to develop in them a larger appreciation of the human family. He planned to be with them individually and as a group. He knew it was essential to have enough men to provide diversity but not so many that they would be unable to develop relationships. Jesus had a right-size school for the purpose he had in mind.

Choosing the Twelve

Jesus was working on an earth-wide, time-long enterprise. He set out to develop a nucleus of men who could carry on when he left. Mark put it fittingly: "He ordained twelve that they should be with him" (3:14). Here was face-to-face association. In his farewell conversation to the eleven, after Judas had left, he said, "I have chosen you and ordained you, that you should go forth and bear fruit" (John 15:16). Jesus stuck to this conviction even when his men wavered. During the crisis in Gethsemane, when they felt it was too dangerous to stay with Jesus, he held to his expectation in them. Even after Peter denied knowing him, he kept faith in Peter and in the others.

Jesus took choosing the twelve very seriously. After continuing all night, he called his disciples together and "of them he chose twelve, whom he called apostles." This was not happenstance; he conferred with his Father. And he wanted these men to realize that God was calling them. He told them that they would have exacting work which sometimes would be extremely dangerous. He told them that they would not be going out alone. God, who called them, would be with them. In times of emergency, God would provide them with what they should say and would guide them with respect to what they should do. Jesus said, "The Spirit of your Father will be speaking through you" (Matthew 10:20). The Holy Spirit would come into the picture in a functioning way, as promised resource.

Twelve Different Persons

These twelve were all Jews, but they were not identical. Dr. William Barclay in *The Master's Men* wrote: "The constitution of the twelve presents us with a situation which is nothing less than a miracle in personal relationships." This diversity reveals how Jesus was concerned not only with reconciling men to God but with reconciling men to each other. Some have said that if these twelve men, so different in temperament and attachments, could live together in harmony, then men of any background should be able to make a go of it. Without the influence of Jesus Christ some of these men might have been at each other's throats.

What an assortment! Very little is said about them, but the following roster stands forth as workable. Each one is provided an identification that the centuries have given. The roster at least will set forth the divergence. This is an illustration of the way the Holy Spirit works with persons in their own patterns of personhood. It does not minister to produce identicals.

1. *Peter, the fisherman, the "rock"*

Through the years, this man has been at the top of most listings of the first apostles. He might be called Simon Peter or Simon Cephas. "Peter" comes from the Greek word for rock and Cephas from the Aramaic. He has been described as impulsive, easily roused to adventure, loyal to the end. Matthew began his list with "First, Simon" (10:2). By this time Peter must have become considered the leader of the apostolic group. He was usually the first to speak up, to declare himself. To him Jesus gave specific commission.

2. *John, the apostle of love*

John and James were sons of Zebedee. Jesus called them "Boanerges...sons of thunder" (Mark 3:17). They must have had some explosive quality in their characters. A trace of this is revealed in what happened when Jesus and the twelve were turning toward Jerusalem after not being well received in one community. James and John blurted out, "Do you want us to call down fire from heaven and burn them up?" John stands out as an example of what can take place when a man of stormy temperament gets with Jesus Christ. He was mellowed but not weakened. Between him and Jesus tradition assigns a close brotherly affection. John and James had a mother with ambitions for her sons; she is pictured as wanting them to have a prominent place in Jesus' new order.

3. *James, the first martyr*

James must have had something of this "thundering" quality, too, although he is often portrayed as "James, the Silent." The picture is given that he sometimes would refrain from saying anything and then burst forth. His blustering way must have been well managed. Herod, apparently wanting to please the Jewish opponents of the disciples, had James executed by sword (Acts 12:2).

4. *Andrew, the man who brought others to Jesus*

Not much is said about Andrew in the New Testament, but what appears is significant. He stands out as the man who brought others to Jesus, including his own brother, Peter (John 1:40-42). He brought the lad with the loaves and fishes (John 6:8-9). He even brought some Greeks to Jesus (John 12:20-22). Although his brother Simon Peter came to the fore, Andrew apparently displayed no trace of resentment.

5. *Thomas, the inquirer*

He has been called "the doubter," but this is hardly fair. He was honest in wanting to find out. The Aramaic Thomas and the Greek Didymus carry the meaning "twin," but no twin brother was ever identified. Perhaps Thomas struck out on his own.

Jesus responded to Thomas as an inquirer, not as a cynical doubter. When Thomas was sure, he believed with intensity.

6. *Matthew, the tax collector*

Matthew, also called Levi, was hated by the Jews because he was a tax-gatherer and thus aligned with the Romans. With other men of the twelve he came with stigma against him. But Jesus saw his integrity and summoned him. It appears that he was doing well in his business, but when Jesus said, "Follow me," he got up at once, left everything behind, and went with him (Luke 5:28). One important thing he took with him was his pen.

7. *Philip, the disciple with practical outlook*

Philip of Bethsaida was identified as the first man to whom Jesus said, "Follow me!" (John 1:43). The next mention of him was made when he brought his good friend Nathaniel to Jesus. Here was revealed the practical turn of this man. He did not discuss Jesus with his friend; he brought Nathaniel to Jesus so he could see for himself. This characteristic was again revealed when he faced the large crowd of people in Galilee. Jesus turned to Philip and asked, "Where shall we buy bread that these may have something to eat?" Philip replied that it would take a lot of money to buy bread so that each person would have even a little. Dr. William Barclay says that Philip's response was something like this, "A year's pay would not buy enough to give this crowd a bite apiece" (page 89). Philip is remembered, too, for what he said that last evening: "Show us the Father, Lord, and we shall be satisfied." Jesus must have been troubled by such a request at so late a date. He replied, "Philip, have you been with me all this while and not come to know me? If you have seen me, you have seen the Father." Philip was a well-meaning, friendly disciple, not an aggressive adventurer.

8. *Nathaniel, Israelite of integrity*

Generally Bartholomew and Nathaniel are thought of as names designating the same person. Foremost stands Jesus' identification, "an Israelite in whom is no guile" (John 1:47). Nathaniel was willing to be convinced when things were not according to his notions (including his notion about Nazareth). He stands forth as a saintly man of deep conviction and loyalty. It is a significant accolade when people today are told that they are like Nathaniel of old.

9. *Simon, the Zealot*

A zealot was a fervent patriot who wanted to oust the Romans from Jewish territory. They might well have been called fanatic Jewish nationalists. Sometimes this apostle was called Simon the Canaanite, which indicates how thoroughly he was associated with the native land. Usually he was referred to as Simon Zelotes. The change in this man's life must have been tremendous as he replaced the sword with saintly service.

10. *Thaddeus, the three-names man*

He was also called Lebbaeus and Jude, the son of James. There is only one mention of him, but this is of consequence. In the conversation period during the Last Supper Jesus was talking about love. Lebbaeus (Jude) broke his accustomed silence and burst forth impulsively, "Lord, how is it that you will manifest yourself to us but not to the world?" Jesus told him that only those who loved in God's way would be able to discern him, for his was the way of love. Jesus went on to point out that the Comforter, the Holy Spirit, would be the coming teacher. The Spirit would teach the way of love. Thaddeus was a man of quality who never pushed to the fore, but who spoke up significantly when he did speak.

11. *James, the son of Alphaeus*

There is no descriptive phrase for this man. Sometimes he is identified as the apostle about whom the least is known. He may have been a brother of Matthew, whose father's name was Alphaeus. And there have been some presumptions that he was a Zealot. If so, he and his brother would have had widely divergent sociopolitical views. Here would have been another miracle of two men getting together with Jesus Christ.

12. *Judas Iscariot, the man with inner dissension and outer infidelity*

This man, often designated as the traitor and betrayer, had other characteristics. At least in his closing moments he suffered anguish and a sense of guilt for what he had done. It has been said that his real sin was that he wanted Jesus to fit into his patterns of what a Messiah should be. What prompted Jesus to choose Judas? Was it to round out the roster of varying types of personalities? Was he to serve as a prototype when, at later time, chosen men would go astray?

There were many contrasts in this company of twelve: Matthew the Publican *vs.* Simon the Zealot; the loquacious Peter *vs.* the silent James; the trusting

John *vs.* the searching Thomas; the betraying Judas Iscariot *vs.* the guileless Nathaniel. The Good Spirit invites all types.

Conversations and Conferences

In Jesus' laboratory school he and his men would talk together. Some times they would plan ahead for such occasions. There was two-way speaking and listening. Jesus did not have bulletins and broadcasts. He and his men looked one another in the eye. Much of what we call communication today is not communication; it is "monomunication." Jesus lived with his disciples intimately enough that barriers were dissolved.

This ease of approach is illustrated in their request that he teach them to pray. They had caught something of the vitality of his prayers. He did not employ conventional, liturgical phrases but talked things over with his Father. When they requested, "Lord, teach us to pray," he used language meaningful to them, starting with a significant salutation: "Our Father." He prompted them to express their spiritual community as they said, "Our." Recently a Roman Catholic priest said, "Forgive me when I say Our Father and do not mean it." But in South Africa, where racism divides, it is reported that a directive went out from the white overseers to the black children, advising them to leave out the word "Our." Jesus led his men in praying together. They were to have fraternal communion with God. When he taught them about praying, it was not yet time to speak to them about the Holy Spirit. This would come later.

133

On their final night together there was exchange; there were questions. When Jesus said that he was leaving, Peter immediately asked, "Where are you going?" (John 13:36). Thomas followed with, "How can we go with you when we do not know which road you are going to take?" (John 14:5). Jude ben Alphaeus came up with his question about Jesus' refraining from showing himself to the world. When Jesus spoke of the betrayal, John asked forthrightly, "Lord, who is it?" (13:25). Jesus stimulated his men to ask questions that mattered. He was getting them ready for the ministering of the Holy Spirit. He was wanting them to see the relationship between sound interrogation and sound inspiration. They would commune with the Spirit as with him.

And Jesus was ever holding conferences with his men. The basic meaning of confer is "to carry together." Some think of the essence of conference as the holding of business meetings. There can be many business meetings with little carrying together. Those who confer have to be doing something together so they will have something to carry together. Conferers say "we." Jesus taught his men to include God in their conferring. A vital church ever associates the guiding of the Holy Spirit with searching for the way to go. Revelation has come when the Saints have been truly conferring, carrying together, searching together.

Sometimes Jesus would take his disciples apart from the crowd so they would be able to commune and confer. There is a limit to the number that can participate in a conference. He would take them away that they might return to their work with more insight, more inspiration. Prior to that last conference Jesus directed two of his men to arrange for a place where they might commune. He wanted to teach them about the ministry of the Holy Spirit. He wanted them to experience this Spirit. Jesus talked about his own relations with them and with his Father. He went to their world of personal experience for such a conversation.

Reporting and Reviewing

After Jesus had lived with his apostles long enough and closely enough that they had absorbed something of his mission and message he sent them out to minister. They went where the people were. They went about "preaching the gospel and healing everywhere" (Luke 9:6). Then they came back to report. Luke made this summary statement: "And the apostles returned and told Jesus what they had done" (9:10). For their own sake Jesus wanted them to go over what they had done.

This was a first-class conference. "He took them and withdrew into a desert place by the city of Bethsaida." The gist of what they said was something like this: "We could do more than we ever thought we could." They had a sense of empowerment. Now the apostles could talk about things for which they had not been ready hitherto. Now Jesus could ask them, "Who do men say that I am?" and "Who do you say that I am?" Peter with his customary forthrightness answered, "You are the Christ, the Son of the living God" (Matthew 16:16). One of the foremost affirmations in history, this took more than a knowledge of

135

linguistics—it took the voice of experience. Then, "He charged his disciples to tell no one that he was the Christ" (16:20). The people would have heard this and interpreted it in their own ways. What Jesus had in mind in his Christship was not the usual line of thinking.

This sending out of witnessing workers continued. Luke wrote how Jesus appointed "other seventy" and "sent them on ahead of him, two by two, unto every town and place where he himself would come." He sent them as his ambassadors, saying, "He who receives you receives me" (Matthew 10:40). In time these "other seventy" returned to report "with joy" (Luke 10:17), and Jesus was happy with them. Luke wrote: "In the same hour he rejoiced in the Holy Spirit." "Blessed are the eyes that see what you see" (Luke 10:23), Jesus said privately to his men. Others would not have understood. He did not talk about the Holy Spirit in crowds or about his Messiahship to the masses. He spoke about these things with those who had experienced the Holy Spirit in their laboratory work with God.

Jesus never threw testimony about here and there. Instead, he built a background so those who heard would get what he meant.

Transfiguration and Transformation

A man of the plains was standing a few miles from the Rocky Mountains for the first time. It was a cloudy day and he saw little. "I've heard so much about these mountains," he said, "but frankly there's not much to see." The next morning, when he looked again, the sun was shining...and the man gazed in wonder. He saw peaks, valleys, pine trees, clouds, and color shadings. After a while he commented, "Something has happened to them. And now something is happening in me." A friend who had been with him the day before made no comment at first. Then he reflected, "Things certainly look different when light shines on them." This is what happens in *transfiguration*. The Light shines and persons are changed. It is like what happened in the man when he saw the sunlit mountains. This is what happens in *transformation*.

Jesus' disciples needed to see things—and *him*—in the light. These twelve men had been viewing their world and their master against their own backgrounds, in their own light. Sometimes the setting was cloudy. These men were Jews, and they saw God as all Jews had been taught to view him. Jesus wanted them to "look to the mountains" and see with larger light.

Continuing to talk about light, Jesus said, "As long as I am in the world, I am the light of the world" (John 9:5) and "I give unto you to be the light of the world." This was not traditional light. If Jesus had exuded a sun-like brilliance from his body, many would have said, "He is the Messiah." They wanted visible signs. But what Jesus referred to was the spiritual glow that would transform his disciples. And when they really got in the transfiguring light, they *were* transformed. They became different men.

Jesus lived with his men with awareness that what he wanted to happen in their lives would require longer time. A graph would show many ups and downs in their lives as they went along with him in their laboratory school. Here is a list of major trends in their lives during those days:

1. *Extension of time and influence in things that were to take place in God's program.* The all-of-a-sudden outlook was giving way to intent to work with God a longer time.

2. *Emphasis on inner insight and awareness with understanding rather than upon external signs and wonders.*

3. *The worth of all persons in the sight of God.* This included those who had been disregarded or denounced. The role of children was stressed. Gentiles were coming into the circle of God's concern—also publicans and Samaritans.

4. *Blessedness interpreted as happiness that came through co-working and co-loving with God in outreach to others.* For many, to be blessed had meant to receive favors. Jesus' beatitudes set forth spiritual qualities.

5. *Insight into the wholeness of life, the wholeness of personhood, the wholeness of the gospel.* Jesus kept saying, "Be whole."

6. *Achievement of spiritual excellence and competency through continuing growth.* Jesus ever conversed with his men about bearing fruit.

7. *Spiritual priority through quality of character, notably through free giving of one's self for the welfare of others.* Ranking in office and gradations through priestly positions and the like were not in Jesus' program.

8. *Appreciation of diversities between persons with*

awareness of the possibilities of achieving harmony through living together with Jesus Christ.

9. *Awareness of the divinity of Jesus Christ through living with him and sensing the divine quality in his life, in his person.*

10. *A sense of the influence on their lives as a result of being with Jesus and catching his radiant influence.*

11. *Elemental perception of what Jesus meant by "light."* Seeing this in terms of insight and inspiration enabled them to see God's way.

12. *Initial awareness of the Holy Spirit and of the type of ministering it was to bring into their lives.*

In the laboratory school of Jesus Christ learning was explored through living with him. He combined theory and practice, evaluation and interpretation with exploration and experimentation. He taught theology in such a way that as the men grew in readiness they were given more mature concepts.

Laboratory schools with Jesus Christ are needed today as then. In these schools exploring learners find out about the Holy Spirit in actual life situations. They discover its light-affording and life-furthering ministries. They learn to tap the resources of the Good Spirit.

Jesus
Promised
Spiritual Endowment

Jesus Christ was always living in the present—always directing the immediate today into a worthy tomorrow. He did this superbly while he was with his disciples. He was always guiding them in present exploration and future expectation. He spoke to them about what was coming. This gave purpose and direction and vitality to what they were doing that very day. He wanted them to be working rather than worrying or wishing. He warned them against speculating about the end of time.

Jesus talked to his men in their language. This involved more than mere vocabulary. He talked with them in their own cultural setting. His illustrations and his parables were based on the world that they knew. Today we have to reconstruct this Jewish world in order to appreciate and understand Scripture. This can be difficult but unless we do, much of what we read in the Bible lacks meaning.

This language of the apostles included their ideas,

their feelings, their values, their personhood. Jesus sensed their limitations and their loyalties and their likes. On that closing evening he said frankly, "I have many things to say unto you, but you cannot bear them now" (John 16:12). Jesus shared with them as much as they could grasp. They would need a larger world of experience to understand and appreciate what he would be saying. Many amateurs in their study of Jesus and their interpretation of the Holy Spirit are inclined to comment, "God can do anything." Others are inclined to add, "When the Holy Spirit comes to a man, he can grasp anything." Jesus did not talk this way. He wanted his disciples to mature, to increase in their potentials, so they would be able to perceive what he was trying to teach them. God always wants his sons and daughters to increase their capacity and responsiveness that he might reveal more to them.

A New Teaching in an Old Language

When it came time for Jesus to tell the apostles that he was going to leave them, he faced a difficult situation. He had to prepare them for the shock. They were still anticipating a triumphant Messiah who would conquer their anti-Jewish enemies. There was little or no place for the Holy Spirit in their Messianic pictures. Jesus had to reconstruct prevailing notions about the Messiah and put this in new language.

Jesus saw the need to release these men from their loyalties to him and to look toward the Holy Spirit as their minister after his departure. But they were not used to thinking or talking about the Holy Spirit. Their

141

questions and comments at the Last Supper showed how limited they were in this field. If they could see what Jesus had been doing, they would be able to apply this to the Holy Spirit. What he was going to say to these men about the Holy Spirit he had already said in his life, in his personhood—something very hard to put into words. Those who wrote the New Testament had the almost impossible task of trying to describe this in the Greek language.

That Last Evening Together

When Jesus met his men in the Upper Room, he told them that he had wanted very much to eat this Passover Supper with them. What he did that evening expressed his deep concern and his affection for them. First, they ate the meal together. In those lands eating together constituted a pledge of mutual consideration. At the close of the meal, he blessed and served the bread and wine. This was an expression of covenant and remembrance. He washed their feet, as only a loving host would do. He pointed out the line between fidelity and infidelity when he singled out Judas and opened the way for him to leave. Only the faithful were included in the conversation that followed in which Jesus got at the heart of things. Here he told them about the work of the Holy Spirit.

Jesus moved on and up in his heart-to-heart conversation. He had been making his school a community of comrades. He had expressed day by day with his men the love that he was going to talk about. In reporting on this evening, John used the Greek word *agape* to denote the kind of love Jesus was

142

expressing. This was more than sentimentality or physical indulgence; it was love of a spiritual quality. Jesus expressed it so succinctly when he said, "This is my commandment, that you love one another, as I have loved you." He told them he was laying down his life for them and for all others, but at that time they did not comprehend what he meant.

Jesus led up to this climactic statement: "You are my friends. Henceforth, I am not calling you servants. The servant does not know what his master is doing." Then he told them how he had been sharing with them what his Father had shared with him. This was one of the high moments in their consociation.

Jesus went on to point up some tests of their friendship that would come in a few hours. They would desert him. Peter would deny him. But there would be recovery and restoration. They would find him again, expand their friendship through the ministering of the Holy Spirit. He wanted them to see that genuine friendship was more than a momentary experience; it required foundation.

Jesus did not theorize or use high-sounding phrases or doctrinal concepts. He spoke in ways that his disciples would understand. He did not talk about the "Holy Trinity" or the "blessed Trinity." These phrases came later. He spoke in simple language about the personal presence of the Holy Spirit that would minister to them as he had been doing.

The Comforter

Jesus had to use some term that would identify this promised Presence. He spoke, of course, in his native tongue. When John wrote the account in Greek he used the word *Paracletos*. Sometimes this is translated Advocate or Counselor, but the most familiar translation is Comforter. In Ferm's *Encyclopedia of Religion*, Dr. E. F. Scott mentions several translations of the word and then concludes, "The old rendering 'Comforter' is still the best one, when taken in its sense of 'strengthener.'"

What Jesus said about the Holy Spirit occurs in his after-supper conversation with his apostles. The following quotations constitute his foremost teachings, his vital promises about this Spirit:

I am going away from you.

I will pray the Father, and he will send you another Comforter, that he may abide with you forever, the Spirit of truth.

The world cannot receive this Spirit, because they do not see or know him; but he dwells in you and shall be in you.

I will not leave you comfortless.

If a man love me, he will heed my words, and my Father and I come to him and will abide in him.

The Comforter, who is the Holy Spirit, will teach you all things, and will bring things to your remembrance.

When I go away, the Comforter will come to you. . . . He will reprove the world of sin, of unrighteousness.

I have many things to say unto you, but you are not ready to hear them. When the Spirit of truth is come, he will guide you into all truth.

When the Comforter comes to you . . . he shall testify of me; and you shall bear witness, because you have been with me.

Your sorrow shall be turned into joy. Your heart shall rejoice, and no man can take this joy from you.

Let not year heart be troubled. Be of good cheer.... You shall have peace.

I have chosen you and ordained you, that you shall go forth and bring forth fruit. And I shall go with you.

A Source of Strength

The root syllable of the word "comfort" indicates its original meaning—"strength." The prefix "com" or "con" means with or together. Thus comfort denotes strength as there is togetherness. The implication here is that the person will have strength when he is "together with God." Through the years comfort has often taken on the weaker connotation of expressing sympathy. In this sense comfort would be extended to those who were not feeling well or for whom things were not going right. Thus many believers thought of the Spirit coming in times of distress and defeat and death.

Jesus used the word "comforter" in a strong sense. He told his apostles that they were to do demanding work. Sometimes the going would be rough; sometimes the opposition would be direct and hostile. Their work would require stamina. They would need the Holy Spirit as their source of strength. That evening in the Upper Room Jesus told them that the Father would give them "another Comforter" (John 14:16). This would enable them to stand straight and square their shoulders for the work to be done. It would give them courage, reinvigoration, and renewal.

The Holy Spirit was promised by Jesus to those with receptivity for receiving it. God does not give his resources to those who merely want to put on an act of doing things, to have a thrill, or to have something to talk about. The person who prays for the coming of the Holy Spirit needs to have something in mind that is worthy of empowerment for getting the work accomplished.

Jesus never set forth perfection as a requisite for receiving the Holy Spirit, but he expected the person who was helped to devote his improved condition to help bring "abundant" living to others. When Jesus talked to his disciples about the coming of the Holy Spirit, he was commissioning them to go out and "bring forth fruit" (John 15:16). The endowment of the Comforter was to enable them to do this.

Taught by the Spirit

Wherever Jesus was with his apostles he was a teacher. Many times he would say, "You have heard . . . but I say unto you." His teachings had to do with the real business of living. The Spirit who was to come after him would have to be a teaching presence: "The Holy Spirit will teach you all things" (John 14:26). This "all things" statement is thoroughly inclusive. There is no restriction to scriptural quotations and doctrinal phrasings. It ranges from agronomy to zoology, from atoms to zeniths, from Aaron to Zephaniah. And the teaching would be done in the method of Jesus, who always considered the learning resources of the student.

Sometimes there has grown up and spread the notion that teaching through the Holy Spirit means that the recipient can benefit without searching, without preparing, without thinking. Some have used the statement of Luke (12:12) to substantiate this view. Jesus was telling his men that if they came to a time when immediate help was needed, this help would be forthcoming; the Spirit would teach them. Recently a man confessed, "I would like to be taught and directed by the Holy Spirit. Then I would not need to study. I would not need to worry whether what I would say would be right." He felt that words, not thoughts, would be given him.

The way of teaching through the Holy Spirit is the way of teaching that Jesus of Nazareth used with his disciples. He had them search, select, and then speak.

Brought to Remembrance

The word "remembrance" carries significance. A wise counselor has said that we cannot remember what has never been in our experience. This further counsel follows: (1) We are to select what we are going to remember. (2) We are to coordinate what we are going to remember so there will be a correlation. (3) We are to link these remembrances in a functional way to our ongoing working with God. So we qualify to remember. In this way we cultivate utility and efficiency. Then we are entitled to have the Holy Spirit to call to remembrance. During the Last Supper Jesus linked doing with remembering. He said, "Do this in remembrance of me."

His promise that we might have ministry in remembering has received some strained interpretations and applications. A minister in a Pentecostal group wanted to preach "powerfully." He said that the main thing he did was to memorize scripture. He did not need to inquire about the meaning or the application. He just committed to memory the quotations he considered would express power. Then he would relax and "trust the Spirit" to bring to his mind the choice quotations in rapid sequence. He said, "The Spirit will put the punch where it ought to be." When asked if he had any central thought to his message, he replied very frankly that when he had the Spirit he did not need to think. All he needed was to have these scriptures "brought to remembrance"—the Spirit would convincingly carry his quotations to hearers.

When Jesus quoted scripture he did more than repeat past sayings. He looked to meanings and to results application of the scripture would bring in daily living. This happened in the synagogue meeting in Nazareth, his own hometown. He quoted from Isaiah, "The Spirit of the Lord is upon me." When he gave interpretation and application to this scripture that did not suit the villagers, they rose up in wrath and wanted to throw him over the brow of the hill. Jesus always had qualified his quotations, calling for insight, foresight, and oversight in seeing the whole of things. This was more than remembering catalogued statements out of the past; it was providing foundation for continuing divine direction.

Continued Testimony

Testifying had a high place in Jewish culture and religion. It took reliable witnesses to attest the guilt or the innocence of a person in Jewish law. Jesus referred to a standard Jewish view: "In the mouth of two or three witnesses shall every word be established" (Matthew 18:16). False witnessing was severely condemned. It was in good Jewish pattern when Jesus called his disciples to be witnesses. He identified John the Baptist's calling as that of bearing witness of the Light (John 1:7). He insisted that his disciples live so they would have ample vital experience for witnessing. Their testimony was to be more than secondhand reports, hearsay, legend, or graphic headlines. It was to come out of well-authenticated happenings in the lives of persons. He considered them qualified to testify when something transforming happened in their lives. Physical healing without soul healing would not make a worthy testimony. One day Jesus enjoined a man to go among his own people and testify. This man had been troubled with "an evil spirit." He had been confused and obnoxious. Now he was healed, clean, and rightly dressed. Now he was "in his right mind." The man wanted to go along with Jesus, but Jesus advised him, "Go home to your friends and tell them how much the Lord has done for you and how he has had mercy upon you" (Mark 5:19). Here the changed condition of the man himself was a testimony. His words would add to this testimony.

Jesus wanted testimony to be kept up-to-date and to continue after his departing. There was to be more than retelling the story of what happened when he was on earth. One day a little girl, after listening to her mother narrate a moving story out of the Bible, commented, "Mother, God used to do the most exciting things. Why doesn't he do them anymore?"

Jesus did not intend for the "exciting things" to come to an end. Every day of his life something happened that carried testimonial quality. He intended for the Good Spirit to keep things happening; his disciples who experienced this dynamic Spirit were to keep testifying of his work.

Many believers have wanted some fiery experience which would enable them to say, "I testify that Jesus is Christ." Some would like to see the fiery words, "Jesus lives!" written across the sky. Jesus wanted his men to live with him so they would sense his divinity. Now he wanted them to live with the Holy Spirit so they would be able to testify out of the things it would bring to pass. This kind of testimony would come out of seasoned, sound experience of Spirit-empowered living. Jesus might well have told his eleven apostles: "Permit the Holy Spirit to bring to pass in your lives things that will give you vital testimony of my working in lives here and now."

These are the ministries through the Holy Spirit that Jesus set forth that closing night. These are things that would take place in the lives of the eleven and other disciples:

1. In loving God, in loving others, in cultivating true "agape" love.

2. In teaching things of worth.

3. In bringing to remembrance things of worth.

4. In guiding in saintly endeavors.

5. In drawing and stimulating toward reconciliation, repentance.

6. In strengthening saints in Christ-quality service.

7. In testifying of Christ and of his way.

8. In furthering unity among disciples and those inclined Godward.

9. In cultivating friendship with Christ, with Christ's friends.

10. In bringing to pass oneness and peace within the person.

11. In calling out, in commissioning in worldwide field.

12. In experiencing joy of eternal quality.

Preparation

After his resurrection Jesus continued to instruct, to inspire his chosen about the ministering of the Holy Spirit. He told them that there was more preparation to be made. His word was definite and hopeful: "Tarry in Jerusalem until you are endowed with power from on high" (Luke 24:49). Right away the men heeded what he said. They returned from the Mount of Olives to Jerusalem. But these waiting disciples did not sit down and dream about the coming endowment. They kept busy. Very soon they held a conference—a good-sized congregation for such a conference: "About a hundred and twenty" (Acts 1:15). What they did indicated that they expected their movement to continue. Matthias was named apostle to fill the vacancy left by Judas. They were getting ready. The time was urgent for the endowment of the guiding Spirit. They were relying on the promise of Christ Jesus.

Realization
On the Day
Of Pentecost

Pentecost . . . Pentecostal! What a range of meanings
these words have! When they are mentioned,
something favorable or unfavorable pops into the
minds of those who have any conversance with
religion past and present. Here is a common contrast.
To one person Pentecost was the day, a short while
after Jesus left Earth, on which the Holy Spirit came.
To another, Pentecost designates revival meetings with
lots of verbal and gesture expressions. The first tends to
be historic, the second histrionic. In Europe Pentecost
may refer to a holy day, but more than likely to a
holiday. To many the word is merely associated with
religious persons.

Impressions of that first Day of Pentecost in the
Christian story are varied. When the story is read from
the second chapter of the book of Acts one devotee
may emphasize a particular incident of the day, while
another may focus on something else. As explorers we
need to work at finding out as far as possible what

152

happened that day. Then we need to designate with some soundness what should happen on a present Day of Pentecost. We need to see what qualities would characterize the truly Pentecostal person and meeting. We would ask, as searchers did recently, "How does the Holy Spirit behave?" "How would I know that I have the real Spirit?"

The Feast of Weeks

In the calendar of the Jewish year the Passover was regarded as the major event. It was the celebration of deliverance from Egypt—a festival of freedom. Seven weeks later came the Festival of the First Fruits or the Feast of Weeks. Later it took the Greek name, Pentecost, from the fifty days after Passover. This was intended to be a happy occasion. Those original Christian disciples came together in friendly, festival mood to celebrate the gathering of the first fruits of the harvest. Many Jews were in Jerusalem for the day. In time, an additional anniversary was added. It was believed that this was the day on which the Ten Commandments and other laws were given to the Israelites at Mount Sinai, and that the trip from Egypt to Sinai had taken fifty days. How much it was celebrated in this way at the time of Christ is not certain. It is significant that the release from the Law through the coming of the Spirit would take place on the anniversary commemorating the giving of the Law.

Simon Peter must have taken seriously Jesus' directive: "Feed my sheep." It was he who presided in the conference at which the new apostle was selected. The meeting was held in the city where people were able to note what was going on. Peter was in charge. Luke opens his account with this concise statement: "When the day of Pentecost had come, they were all together with one accord in one place." A modern commentator has observed, "In those days they went to the meeting: there was no broadcast from the Jerusalem TV stations of the festival day."

Glossolalia

Glossolalia (speaking in tongues) comes from the Greek word *glossa* (tongue). Since the revival of this phenomenon this is often the first thing that persons associate with the Day of Pentecost. Luke makes no comments, gives no interpretations, but he does include some pretty important aspects on what happened. This is his summary sentence: "They were all filled with the Holy Spirit and began to speak in other tongues, as the Spirit gave them utterance" (Acts 2:4). This attracted the attention of those near the meeting. Onlookers wondered how Galileans could speak in languages other than their own. The group included persons from Mesopotamia to Egypt, strangers from Rome, Jews and proselytes—a cosmopolitan gathering.

This speaking in tongues was more than gibberish. What was said had content. The watchers commented, "We hear them speak in our tongues the wonderful works of God" (2:11). Here was more than emotional utterances. The disciples spoke in existing languages and were saying something.

Pentecost is often set in contrast with Babel (Genesis

154

11). At Shinar the people were going to build a massive tower for two reasons: to get to heaven and to make a name for themselves. Their self-centeredness eventuated in social division and language breakup. After the "confusion of tongues" they became scattered. (It is sad when people cannot speak to one another; this can happen when they have the same national language.) On the Day of Pentecost the disciples understood each other; they had God together. They needed to break through language barriers and cultural fences. Many Jews thought of their God as speaking Hebrew. Some of the "Jewish Christians" thought that a convert should live by Jewish regulations and speak their language. That day the disciples saw how they could surmount these barriers; they experienced a universal fellowship.

George A. Buttrick, in a sermon called "Babel and Pentecost," said that there is "need for a new Pentecost." There is need for men to surmount linguistic barriers and talk together of "the wonderful things of God." Such a Pentecost would not be a repetition of that earlier day. The speaking in tongues would be more than gibberish that said nothing; it would convey gospel. The Holy Spirit might come to enhance and enrich the languages that persons were studying and to connect with the languages of other peoples so they could converse and testify understandingly in their several tongues. These "tongues" might be of various occupations and study specializations as well as differing cultures. A universal fellowship would be furthered, and God would be at the center.

Peter's Preaching

Simon Peter's sermon was the second happening of that day. "Peter, standing with the eleven, lifted up his voice." Peter is usually pictured as having a strong voice; such was needed here. His salutation included both the "men of Judea" and "those who dwell in Jerusalem." It was appropriate that he spoke this way, for his message was thoroughly Jewish. He quoted from two respected Jewish authorities, Joel and David. He spoke of Joel's pointing toward the day when God would pour out his "spirit" with such manifestations as had been witnessed that very day. He referred to David's looking toward the coming of the Messiah. Then he was ready to make his daring affirmation: "This Jesus has God raised up, and of that we are all witnesses" (Acts 2:32). Then he testified that the outpouring of the Spirit which they had been experiencing was what Jesus had promised as the gift from the Father. This was the climactic sentence which Peter burned into the consciousness of his hearers: "Let all the house of Israel know assuredly that God has made him Lord and Christ, this Jesus whom you have crucified" (verse 36). Peter compelled them to make decisions: (1) Do you receive this Jesus as the Christ? (2) If so what are you going to do about it?

Inquiry and Response

The Holy Spirit that accompanied Peter's message was pushing home, impelling action. Luke wrote that the people were "cut to the heart." These inquirers had experienced something of closeness with the disciples.

Moved by God's power, they wanted to know what to do... and they wanted to begin right then.

Peter was direct in his reply; he set forth repentance, baptism, and reception of the Holy Spirit. These were very much in the thinking of the Jews. (1) Repentance, as the turning from self-centered living to the way that lines up with God involves a rectifying process. (2) Baptism is the total aligning with God, with new covenant and new relationship. (3) Reception of the Holy Spirit enables the realigned person to draw on divine power. Peter's message was, "Do these things and good will happen."

Peter's message was more extensive than that included in Luke's account in the book of Acts: "With many other words did he exhort and testify." This should be expected, for these inquirers needed much more than is set forth here. They needed to know what they were getting into—what they were going to be giving their lives to. Peter's closing exhortation was pointed: "Save yourselves from this crooked generation" (verse 40). He was not telling them to separate themselves from all others and apart. Rather he was calling them to rise above the prevailing way of life. Once Moses told his people to do this. They were to look to the God of truth and justice and right, in contrast to the ways of blundering fellow travelers whom he designated as "a perverse and crooked generation" (Deuteronomy 32:4, 5). Peter wanted his hearers to live above the prevailing ways of those about them so they would be able to testify to them and lift them.

A Universal Promise

Peter rose to the heights and reached out fully when he spoke of the promise of the Holy Spirit. What Jesus said must have made an enduring impression. In Galilee, when he gave "the Great Commission" he said, "Go ye into all the world and teach, and I will be with you." This commission closes with the promise of his never failing presence. He wanted his disciples to be able to say, "Christ is here with us!" When he bade them farewell at Bethany (Acts 1) he promised them the Holy Spirit and told them that they should be witnesses in Jerusalem, in Judea, in Samaria, and in all the world.

Peter promised his hearers on the Day of Pentecost that as they would repent and be baptized, they would receive "the gift of the Holy Spirit." Then came the statement: "The promise is to you and to your children and to all that are afar off, every one whom the Lord our God shall call." "Far off" could refer to space, to time, to cultures, to races. Here Peter and his brothers sensed the *universal mission* to which they were assigned.

The Increase

The recording of the baptismal service that followed is brief—but what a sentence it is! "Then they who gladly received his word were baptized: and that same day there were added unto them about three thousand souls." The first word that stands out is "gladly." Seriousness and joy *can* be blended. The other phrase worthy of note is "added unto them." Receiving these newcomers was a small congregation with the twelve apostles as its nucleus. These converts were called to participate with their brothers and sisters in a great enterprise. They would learn more and more that they were in a fellowship of witnesses, of workers, and this fellowship was to have universal quality.

The Witnessing Community

The story of the Day of Pentecost has to include what happened later. There are only six verses at the close of Chapter Two in the book of Acts that tell of the community of Christians in the center place, but they can be read and reread. The account might carry the heading, "The Holy Spirit Builds a Community of Christians."

They met constantly to hear the apostles teach, to have fellowship, to break bread together, to pray together.

All of them felt a sense of awe, as many wonders and signs were done through the apostles.

All those whose faith had drawn them together held everything in common; they sold their possessions and goods, and distributed the proceeds to all, according to the needs of persons.

Day after day they met with one accord in the temple.

They broke bread together from house to house, sharing their meals with gladness and singleness of heart.

They praised God continually, and all the people respected them.

Every day the Lord added to their numbers those who were finding salvation.

Here was a colony of believers whose community life so expressed the good news that others sensed what was happening and joined them.

Another Community in Another Land

Jesus came to the Nephites in ancient America a short while after he left the Jerusalem disciples. The believers in the Western Hemisphere were charged with missionary zeal. They witnessed to their neighbors through the quality of their living together as well as by their spoken word. Peter gave his hearers on the Day of Pentecost in Jerusalem a threefold directive and promise. This same three-emphases invitation must have been given in the New World: "And as many as came to them, and did truly repent of their sins, and were baptized, received the Holy Spirit" (IV Nephi 1:2). This ministering of the Holy Spirit effected transformation in the lives of these believers. They, too, developed a community of mutuality with God at the center. They caught the universal mission of Christ and went out to the Lamanites who had been their enemies through many generations, and these Lamanites responded. Here were some of the qualities in this community of saints:

There were no contentions and disputations among them, and every man did justly with one another.

They had all things common among them: there were neither rich nor poor, bond or free.

And surely there could not be a happier people among all the people who had been created by the hand of God.
—IV Nephi 1:3-19.

The industriousness generated by the gospel brought material prosperity to the disciples. In time, their involvement in these matters drew them from their primary loyalty to Christ. Material wealth took priority over spiritual wealth. Social stratification began to abound, and the erstwhile pentecostal community disintegrated.

Ministry of the Spirit

Jesus had advised his men at his departing that the Holy Spirit would come to equip them for the work that they were to do; they would have power (Acts 1:8). They had to learn how this power was to be expressed and for what purpose. Often the populace wanted "signs and wonders." They wanted blessings that would give them the tangibles they hoped for. Jesus would not stoop to such pressuring. When he effected a healing it was never to get public attention; he healed to help the person to further "abundant living." He emphasized the transforming ministry of the Spirit, not attention-getting miracles.

This came to a head in Galilee the day after he had fed the multitudes. He had done this because the people were hungry and needed food; he did not do it to attract a crowd and make headlines. The next day he sensed that they were coming back for more "free fishburgers." Since he could not build his new spiritual order on such motivation he talked with them about "the living bread" (John 6:51), but the people were not interested in this kind of food. John summarized the outcome: "From that time many of his disciples went back, and walked no more with him" (6:66).

Jesus was endeavoring to build in his men a foundation for perceiving what this spiritual food was. He was looking toward their experiencing the nourishment of the Holy Spirit. They received this in large measure on the Day of Pentecost. They found a new strength.

Universality

That Day of Pentecost the apostles and many disciples rose above their former limited notions. Just before Jesus bade the apostles farewell by Bethany some asked about the time for the restoring of the kingdom. But Jesus pointed them away from speculation about the matter. He must have looked forward to their soul expansion, when they would see beyond their own small world. This happened on the Day of Pentecost.

1. The Spirit-endowed speaking in tongues lifted them above their linguistic fences. Peoples from many lands and languages were able to converse about great things. This pointed them to *universal fellowship*.

2. This companionship of the Holy Spirit pointed toward the *universal Christ*. If Jesus were to be limited to his physical presence, he would minister only to those people with whom he could have his physical presence felt. Now the Spirit would minister to those of many lands at the same time. Jesus could go with them and be with them and minister with them as a universal *Christ*.

3. These disciples saw the outreach of God to persons from various lands. The response of many people to the message, to the call of the day, indicated that those of other countries would hear and answer. Now the disciples could and would go out on a *universal mission*.

A New Criterion

After Pentecost, endowment through the Holy Spirit became the foremost criterion for God-accepted discipleship. Philip went to Samaria and preached with convincing power: "There was great joy in the city" (Acts 8:8). Many were baptized, but their experience was not complete. Peter and John went to Samaria and continued the ministry begun by Philip. These two apostles "prayed that they [these Samaritans] might receive the Holy Spirit.... Then they laid their hands on them, and they received the Holy Spirit." This was a foremost witness of the universality of Christ's gospel; even Samaritans experienced the Holy Spirit. There was something quite detectable in this endowing experience. The sorcerer Simon wanted to purchase the power to bestow this Spirit; thus originated the word "simony" denoting the purchase or misuse of sacred things for profit.

Another expression of this new criterion occurred when Peter was directed to go to Cornelius and his household. This was a strain on Peter, because he did not see how the gospel would go to Gentiles. Then came the confirmation of mission to Gentiles: "While Peter was still speaking, the Holy Spirit came upon those who were listening" (Acts 10:44). The Jews who were with Peter were astounded that Gentiles should receive the Holy Spirit. This provided the validation for baptizing these Gentiles. Peter's own reaction was clear: "Can any man forbid their baptism, when they have received the Holy Spirit?" God was using his Spirit to guide people as well as to confirm them. When Peter returned to Jerusalem his Jewish associates questioned him about baptizing Gentiles. Peter did not argue or quote from the law. Instead, he testified how these Gentiles had experienced the Holy Spirit (Acts 11:15 ff.). This testimony was evidence that God accepted them.

In the conference of Jerusalem A.D. 49 the question of baptizing Gentiles was the main item on the agendum. Peter did not debate. He testified again that these Gentiles had received the Holy Spirit even as those in the conference had, and this statement carried the conference. Paul and Barnabas gave their testimonies, too. Spiritual experience took precedence over legalistic quotings (Acts 15).

When Paul came to Ephesus (Acts 19) he met a few believers who must have seemed somewhat incomplete in their entering into the Christian life. He asked them pointedly, "Have you received the Holy Spirit?" They gave a naïve answer: "We have not heard that there is the Holy Spirit!" So Paul laid his hands on them, and "the Holy Spirit came on them." The promise of Christ, experience in Pentecost, came to pass in following days.

In Later Years

As centuries went by, the Day of Pentecost came to be identified as the occasion when "the outpouring of the Holy Ghost" occurred. More and more the word "Ghost" was replaced by the word "Spirit." This was done to get away from the undesirable connotation of the word "ghost." By the close of the second century Pentecost was established as a day of celebration—no fastings, no kneeling in prayer, no deprivations. Often it was considered a season for baptisms. The large number of converts on that first day suggested this.

Different emphases grew up. W. E. Sangster in *Special-Day Sermons* designates Pentecost as "the birthday of the church for the church was born when the Holy Spirit was given" (page 105). Some who translate *Paraclete* as meaning "the divine Advocate" focus on the Holy Spirit pleading for humanity—then through the regenerated person to others for others. Some stress the expanding work possible through this Spirit. William Noel in Harper's *Bible Commentary* refers to Pentecost as "the beginning of the welding together of mankind into one great family of God by the reconciling power of Christ himself, ascended, but now in Spirit present with his people everywhere forever" (page 122). Pentecostal sects look to the overt expressions that they consider manifestations of the Spirit. These—particularly "the gift of tongues"—are considered as evidence that the person has received "the baptism of the Spirit."

For most Christians the Day of Pentecost became an anniversary on the seventh Sunday after Easter. The "active" sects did not hold so much to any day; they felt that Pentecostal experience could and should occur on any day. In some countries the original holy day has become a holiday. On the whole there has been a dearth in insight about the Holy Spirit and its functional ministering. Often it has come to have little to do with the mission of the church in transforming living. Sound interpretation, wholesome inspiration, and worthy experience concerning the Spirit of Pentecost Day are greatly needed.

Paul Explored
And
Explained

Paul exerted tremendous influence on Christianity after his day. The writings he left were very influential; they came to be accepted as authoritative. There may have been other writings, but Paul's came to the fore. Sometimes it appears that what he said and what those who read his writings have said that he said have not always fully agreed.

The letters of Paul do not constitute a systematic theology. They were written to deal with specific problems in particular situations. For instance, he never wrote a systematic interpretation of the Holy Spirit. He mentioned the Holy Spirit as it related to what was happening in congregations. We have to pick up sections here and there and piece them together. Nowhere did he set forth an organized, inclusive interpretation of the Holy Spirit, but references to the Spirit appear often in his writings. He considered this Spirit indispensable for the good life of the congregation, whether in Corinth or Ephesus. We need to see this undergirding whether or not Paul mentioned the Spirit specifically.

Paul's Three Cultures

When a person speaks of or interprets something such as the Holy Spirit, he has to do so in the words and the concepts available in his own culture. Paul was able to draw on three major cultures in which he was schooled. Born a Jew, he had gone to Jerusalem as a youth to study under the great rabbi Gamaliel. He knew of the Jewish belief in "the breath of life" which God breathes into man. He was at home in Greek society, and his native city of Tarsus was a center of Greek education. His speech on Mars Hill in Athens indicates that he was at home with Greek patterns of thinking. He was also a Roman citizen, having inherited this citizenship from his father. Paul could draw on all these resources when he endeavored to express what the Christian faith meant to him.

Paul's Nature and Experience

Paul was no hyphenated person. He was either for something or against it. The intensity of his own conversion had a strong bearing on the way he reacted to and in the Christian faith. Prior to his acceptance of Christianity he did not merely take a stand against the followers of Jesus; he was "breathing threats and murder" against them. He got permits from priestly officials in Jerusalem to go to Damascus and locate these strange believers so he could "bring them bound." In Luke's writings Christianity is referred to as "the way" for the first time. Later it is capitalized.

After his conversion Paul devoted his full energy to witnessing of "the Way."

Paul's conversion experience on the Damascus road was direct and intense. His experience with Jesus Christ was immediate. He was addressed by his own name: "Saul, Saul, why are you persecuting me?" When Jesus identified himself, a bewildered, stricken Paul responded as directly, "What do you want me to do?" Here was the response of a go-into-action person. Saul was blinded and weak; he did not eat or drink. This confusion and helplessness lasted for three days.

Then came the directive to Ananias in Damascus to go to Saul. It is understandable that Ananias was hesitant. He had heard of Saul's hostility toward Christians. He needed some assurance about this unusual man. Then came the directive, "Go, for he is a chosen instrument of mine to carry my name before the Gentiles and kings and sons of Israel." Here was one of those cases when there would be either a mess or a miracle. Ananias walked to the house where Paul was staying and went directly to him. What he said and did provides foundation for Saul's reactions concerning the Holy Spirit. Laying his hands upon the perplexed man Ananias said, "Brother Saul, the Lord Jesus who appeared to you on the road by which you came, has sent me, that you may regain your sight and be filled with the Holy Spirit" (Acts 9:17). Saul regained his sight immediately. There was no need to wait. He arose and was baptized. He took bread and was strengthened. The Spirit was working miracles in his life. The brotherly ministry of Ananias, the laying on of hands, the receiving of sight, the baptism, and the coming of the Holy Spirit made up a remarkable happening; this was an ensemble of spiritual newness and uplift. He had seen the light; he had been renewed by the life-giving Spirit. He felt that he was a new man...and he was!

The Sustaining Spirit

Paul did not keep writing about the Holy Spirit, but it undergirded him as he wrote about many things. Wheeler Robinson in *The Christian Experience of the Holy Spirit* made this summary affirmation: "The increasing recognition that the doctrine of the Holy Spirit is central in the Christian thought of the Apostle Paul...marks a great advance in the interpretation of his gospel" (page 14). He undergirded his writings with the conviction that the Spirit drew him and foundationed him in his coming to Christ. Sometimes he spoke of the "Spirit," sometimes of "the Spirit of God," sometimes of the "Spirit of Christ," and sometimes of the "Holy Spirit." He was referring to the same Spirit but with different emphases.

What Paul saw in his own encounter he tended to put into the experience of others who found new life in Christ. This stands to the fore in his letter to the saints in Thessalonica. He had been compelled to leave that city as harsh opposition arose (Acts 17). He wondered if these converts to Christ would have the stamina to hold up under severe persecution. When word came that they had held fast, Paul was exuberant. This stirring sentence expressed what he believed about their experience and about his own: "Our gospel came unto you in something more than words; in power, in

169

the Holy Spirit, in much assurance" (1:5). It had holding quality. He was saying that this was the way the gospel came to him. Then he added, "Accepting the message meant bitter persecution, but you experienced the joy of the Holy Spirit." Paul blended joy with assurance.

The Right Approach

Paul wrote his letters so the people of the congregation would get his message. He did not set down a definitized, systematic presentation but responded to questions they asked or to reports that had come to him. Sometimes he wrote out of his conversance with their situation. In his letter to the Corinthian congregation he said, "Brothers, I would like to have you informed concerning spiritual. . . ." The word that follows differs in various translations. The King James version refers to "spiritual gifts"; the Greek Diaglott, "spiritual persons"; the Phillips version, "spiritual matters." Paul was saying that he wanted the saints to be informed about what is termed "spiritual." He was saying that right experiencing of the Holy Spirit was indispensable, and that mis-experiencing would lead to confusion and error. It was not enough that these Corinthian saints believed in and wanted the Holy Spirit; they needed to believe rightly.

It would be quite an experience to have Paul living today and writing to Restoration Saints. He would use the conceptions and explanations of contemporary researchers whenever these would contribute well. He would look to biological, psychological, sociological

170

specialists and more. He would be conversant with studies about man and the universe. One of the qualities of vital religion is that it does not fence in. This applies to explorations of the Holy Spirit. People who believe in revelation will ever be looking for ways to express larger insights. God would be prompting Paul today to talk about the Holy Spirit in the most meaningful and vital language available. As we read Paul's writings to his fellow saints in ancient days we search for the basics that he would carry through and express in today's concepts. And always we would be aware that no language of his day or of our day would be adequate for interpretation of the Holy Spirit.

Excitement or Enlightenment

Paul crossed over into Europe with a deep conviction of mission. In Troy he had heard the call, "Come over into Macedonia and help us." Here he saw the Holy Spirit in action in his life. First he went to Philippi, then to Thessalonica, then to Berea. Hostility required him to leave all of these places. In each, however, he was able to develop a community of believers before he left. Then he went to Athens. There is little or no indication that much happened there in response to his ministry. The people were more inclined toward dialogue than dedication to a cause. In Corinth it was different. Paul stayed in this metropolitan city for eighteen months and a branch of the church took shape. From there he wrote to other congregations. Then from other congregations he wrote back to the saints in Corinth, both on his own initiative and at their request.

171

From Paul's letters to Corinth we get the picture of a congregation that was struggling to discover what the Christian way of living should be. With their background in Greek religion, the Corinthian saints faced many problems. They had to see God as righteous (some Greek deities did not seem affected by moral considerations). They had to see living with God expressed in righteousness. They had to learn how to meet together in group worship that was worthful. They had to see what the Holy Spirit was and how it should function in their everyday living. They had differences over "favorite preachers," over eating patterns, and more.

These recently converted Corinthian Christians were getting excitement and exhilaration through the "manifestations of the Holy Spirit." They enjoyed the external expressions, especially speaking in tongues. It appears that this was considered a major index of "possession by the Spirit," although the inclination seems to have been toward "jabbering without saying anything." Paul brought this matter to the fore and considered with them God's intent for ministry through tongues. He was frank in pointing up that the Spirit was for more than temporary ecstatic excitement; it was for uplifting enlightenment.

Edification

Paul set forth "edification" as the foremost criterion for what was considered spiritual. *Edify* and *edifice* come from the same root meaning "to build up." Paul linked understanding with "edification." He was writing to the Corinthians that where there was edification there was understanding, but so-called spiritual expression without understanding was to be discredited or put on a low scale. This was his counsel: "Since you are eager for manifestation of the Spirit, strive to excel in the edifying of the church" (I Corinthians 14:12). Another translation contains this wording: "Strive to excel in building up the church." Paul made it clear that edifying entails understanding (I Corinthians 14:15-17). In his second letter he spoke very frankly to these members. He wrote how much he loved them and wanted to help them. He rounded out his letter with this testimonial statement about himself and Titus, whom he had sent to them: "We do all things, beloved, for your edifying." (Another translation makes it read "for your upbuilding.") He finished his counsel with this injunction: "Let all things be done unto edification" (I Corinthians 14:26).

Paul saw the situation realistically. He understood what these Corinthians were doing. He did not turn cynical or negative. He did not treat their practices with disdain. He might have denounced speaking in tongues; instead he called the saints to desire more meaningful expressions of the Spirit. He applied this to their meetings, including their music. They were to sing "with understanding" (I Corinthians 14:15). His counsel was inclusive: "Let all things be done decently and in order" (I Corinthians 14:40).

Pauline Principles

From Paul's writings these principles stand out with clarity. He wanted disciples to catch hold of these and

173

get ready for the edifying ministry of the Holy Spirit.

1. The Holy Spirit has wide range of expression.

2. It ministers suitably to the given person. Initiative and individuality are respected and utilized.

3. The "manifestation of the Spirit is given to every man to profit withal." Here profit signifies "to fit for"—to fit for participation in God's work. The Spirit develops man for good.

4. The Holy Spirit furthers communion with Christ, affording assurance and conviction of the reality and availability of Christ.

5. The Spirit effects fraternity and harmony in the relationship with those who experience it. This unity centers in the Giver of the Spirit.

6. The Holy Spirit edifies persons and groups, building them up in understanding, in steadfastness, in charity.

Endowment by this Spirit effected uplift and insight and outreach in the Corinthian congregation, as it can in any congregation. Persons so endowed get concerned with major things. They get together in mutual support. They want to share the gospel with others. The living, loving Christ draws them together in fruitful, spiritual living. Paul affirmed that the man who is so endowed becomes a new creation (II Corinthians 5:17 ff.). He becomes a different person.

Fruitage with Wide Diversity

Paul used a practical pattern of thinking to set forth how the Holy Spirit functions in the life of a person. He said the Spirit promotes fruit-bearing. Jesus had spoken to his men in this vein. He spoke of preparing the soil, of planting the seed, of cultivating, and of bringing forth fruit.

We visualize an apple tree. Roots go into the soil. The tree drinks in the light and the warmth of the sun which come from 93,000,000 miles away. The tree lives and bears fruit. This has its parallel in humanity. In the universe are spiritual resources. If the person has the capacity, inclination, and quality to receive this spiritual energy he too can be productive.

Saints are commissioned to plant spiritual seeds and to help the growing process continue. Here the example of Johnny Appleseed bears mention. For fifty years John Chapman of Massachusetts led a nomadic life. He spent most of his time in the Ohio River Valley where he distributed apple seeds to all he met. In time he pruned the trees that came forth. It is estimated that most of the orchards in four states of this valley region owe their origin to Johnny Appleseed. Seeds in right setting can do wonders. This applies to spiritual seeds also.

Paul listed the fruits of the Spirit. This was no finalized classification, but it was an indicative list: love, joy, peace, patience, kindness, faithfulness, etc. He went on to say that the Spirit produces in human life these attributes against which nothing in the Law can strike. He was telling the Galatian saints that the life of a disciple of Christ is fruit-bearing (Galatians 5:22-23).

A story comes from England of a dreamer who entered a spacious store in which the gifts of God were kept. Behind the counter was an angel. The would-be

175

purchaser said, "I have run out of the fruits of the Spirit. Will you restock me?" When the angel hesitated, the dreamer burst out, "I need spiritual fruits, and I need them now." Then the angel behind the counter replied, "We do not stock fruits. We keep only seeds."

Special Gifts

The Saint is to look to developing "spiritual fruits." Paul indicated in his letter to the Corinthians that there are also "spiritual gifts." Man does not ask or beg for these; they are special grants of God. It is sound to think of "spiritual gifts" as "extra" endowment to a person who has spiritual fruitage in this direction. They are granted because there is need and because the recipient has the foundation and the fitness for them. John Garver used to say that he had never heard of a fool being granted the gift of wisdom, but he had seen persons who showed "good common sense" and "right judgment" increase through special endowment. In the lives of the recipients some contributive "exercising" for such a gift was required. The mature person does not petition for these gifts; he leaves the bestowal to God and recognizes the responsibility in "exercising" them.

Paul used terms meaningful to his fellow members. (We wonder what listing he would make today in writing to a contemporary congregation.) Here was the list he gave in his Corinthian letter: wisdom, knowledge, faith, healing, miracles, prophecy, discernment, tongues, interpretation of tongues. And then he placed the gift of love to the fore. He rounded out his message by saying that God grants these gifts as expedient for the edification of his people.

Charismata

Basically this word means "things freely given." Paul used it to denote the new gifts, the added energies that could come to Christians through the Holy Spirit. In writing about "spiritual gifts" in his first letter to the Corinthians (Chapter 12) he used the Greek word *charismata* (the singular is charisma) for gifts. He set forth that a person's natural powers are enlarged and refined and increased in competency as the Spirit ministers. Love, he affirmed, was the highest kind of "charisma."

This word has suffered through popularizing. The adjective "charismatic" has been coined and is used in connection with persons whose natural gifts make them charming or appealing. To the degree that they are able to draw and sway others they are described as "charismatic." This is a cheap application of a basic meaning. The use carries the same general designation as the word "personality." The person who is able to attract others is considered to be charismatic.

Paul used *charismata* to denote "spiritual gifts" that God bestowed. These would come into a person's life through the ministering of the Holy Spirit. This Spirit would make the disciple "charismatic."

The Grace of God

Paul used the word "grace" quite generously. The Greek for grace was *charis,* and the connection with "charisma" was apparent. For Paul, grace was God's

177

love in action toward man—not some theological abstraction or some generalized force. It was dynamic; it was gracious God ever doing something good for man. To Paul the height of divine graciousness was expressed in the voluntary coming of Jesus Christ to earth, in the giving of himself to man for man's good. Such grace rises above legal conceptions and regulations.

Paul could write of grace in this way, for he sensed how God had taken the initiative and reached out to him. He sensed God's patient, vital, continuing concern. He saw that when the Holy Spirit comes into a person's life, that person becomes gracious.

As the Christian movement developed doctrine makers conceived that grace was the power God gave to man. Sometimes the Holy Spirit received little attention, and grace was given emphasis—a view not sustained in Paul's writings. Occasionally the Ephesian letter is used to substantiate the view that grace is God's power given to man. Here grace is seen as a spiritual outcome—as fruit developing in persons out of the giving of divine power in love. Grace is God's loving inclination *toward* man. The Holy Spirit is God's living endowment *in* man. Both the divine favor (grace) and the divine strengthening power (the Holy Spirit) are needed.

New Life in Christ

Paul never had any disposition to postpone living until some future time. He urged his followers to seek "abundant living" then. He felt that when he got with Jesus Christ frustrations gave way to freedom and inner conflict gave way to harmony. In this spirit he wrote to the saints at Philippi, "This one thing I do" (Philippians 3:13). And he could say, "I forget those things which are behind me and I press forward to the things that are before me." He wrote of "the high calling of God in Christ Jesus." His foremost presentation of this conviction is in the eighth chapter of his letter to the Romans.

Paul was convinced that man separated from God was in a bad way. When anything, including the human body, was at enmity with God, there was evil. He wrote that through Christ the man alienated from God could be reconciled to God and become a new creation (II Corinthians 5:17 ff.). Such a person would have a new realization as an adopted son of God. He would have freedom, and purpose for living. Paul came forth with his majestic testimony: "As many as are led by the Spirit of God, they are the sons of God" (Romans 8:14).

Through this Spirit man comes to know the Christship of Jesus. This is basic in Paul's gospel. Man might know facts, theories, or ceremonies about Christ but never know Christ as friend and redeemer. Paul was implying that a person has to live personally with another in order to know him as a person. He wrote, "No man can say that Jesus is the Christ but by the Holy Spirit" (I Corinthians 12:3). Through the centuries that have followed, this statement has received applications that would not square with Paul's thinking. Ever so many people have presumed that this meant some sudden exposure, some sign or wonder of a moment, as requisite for this knowledge.

The total setting carries the view that a person lives and continues to live with Christ through the ministering of the Holy Spirit. Paul implies that the person needs to develop spiritual fruits which will enable him to perceive Christship. This knowing comes through living with Christ.

Vitality and Unity in the Church

Paul wrote letters during his imprisonment in Rome. This was his way of ministering to the congregations he had initiated. He never diminished his emphasis on the life-giving function of the Spirit. Up to this time he had often applied this ministry to a specific congregation, such as the one at Ephesus. Now he spoke of the inclusive church on general mission. He imaged it as a body that required life-affording power. He affirmed: "There is one body and one Spirit" (Ephesians 4:4). He said that the whole body should be "fitly joined together"—something the Holy Spirit was designed to do.

In the years that followed, Paul saw church administrators concerned about unity. They wanted harmony. How were they going to go about achieving this oneness? Were they going to look to the Holy Spirit to bring it to realization?

The Church
Became
Institutionalized

After the first century of the new Christian movement something happened in the field of the Holy Spirit. (It might be more appropriate to say that something did not happen.) Previously the Holy Spirit had become more of a story or a doctrine in a creed or the topic of a rite in the observances of the church. After a century or so the church became increasingly institutionalized, and the Holy Spirit came to be thought of as a phase of the functioning of this organization.

The book of Acts may be called the story of Spirit-led Christians. This Spirit called new ministers who would lead out with vitality and courage. Such was the calling of Barnabas and Saul at Antioch (Acts 13:2). The Spirit directed apostles and others to move out into new mission fields. On such a directive Paul crossed over into Europe, into Macedonia. This Spirit sustained disciples when they were imprisoned because of their faith. So were Paul and Silas delivered in

181

Philippi. This Spirit functioned in healing the breach in the Jerusalem conference (Acts 15) when the young church could have been split in two. The Spirit effected the sanctioning of admitting Gentiles without their being required to fully comply with Jewish laws. It enabled Christians to have firsthand testimony about the Christship of Jesus. It also prompted men to write what became the first books of the New Testament. And the story might go on.

The Second Century

By the opening of the second century other trends developed. No second book of Acts was written. If such a book had materialized by the third century it could hardly have been titled "The Acts of the Apostles." It might have been called "Management by the Bishops." What happened in these decades is summarized by Williston Walker in his *History of the Christian Church*. The sense of immediacy of Christ's return diminished. Hopes were projected farther into the future. This is Dr. Walker's summary:

> In most of the churches of the second century the early hope of the return of Christ was growing dim. The consciousness of the constant inspiration of the Holy Spirit, characteristic of the Apostolic Churches, had also largely faded. With this declining sense of the Spirit's present work came an increased emphasis on His significance as the agent of revelation. The Spirit had been the inspiration of prophecy in the Old Testament. He guided the New Testament writers.—Page 55.

Emphasis turned toward what had happened in the past. In the outlook of many churchmen the sufficiency of these prophetic occurrences in years gone by diminished the need for current Spirit-inspired message and ministry. More and more that which was written in the past came to be considered, as one commentator put it, "diffused and done."

Montanism

As would be expected, now and then there was an attempt to return to the days and the ways of "immediate inspiration." One such initiator was Montanus of Asia Minor. About 156 Montanus heralded himself as the passive instrument through which the Holy Spirit was speaking. This meant that he and his followers believed God took over and their own human powers did not function. This kind of inspiration was set forth to assert the completeness of their spiritual possession. Two prophetesses joined him in his proclamations. They declared that a new dispensation of the Holy Spirit was at hand, that the end of the world and the coming of Christ would soon transpire. With this went strong emphasis on repentance and revival. These "spokesmen for the Spirit" denounced the evils of the times and the worldliness of the Church. They called men to live with self-denial, such as abstinence from meat. They advocated fasting and celibacy. For a time many adherents followed.

But the end did not come. The messages of the "spokesmen" contained less that was specific. Appeal declined. In time Montanism ceased as a movement. Its call to denial in living continued in the church, notably in monasticism. The timing appealed to standing in the hereafter rather than for deliverance at the "second coming." The way of the Spirit, as set forth by Montanus, was limited and was limiting. He and his followers did not look to living, but to the closing out of life. The call of the Spirit with their motivation did not take hold.

Gnosticism

A movement began in the middle of the second century that exerted considerable influence on the life of Christians in matters of spiritual inspiration. It was called Gnosticism and took its name from the Greek word *Gnosis*, which carried the general meaning of "knowledge." Thus a gnostic was a person who said that he *knew*, while an *agnostic* said that he did not know. These Gnostics asserted the need for special spiritual knowledge, but they believed that not many would qualify for this higher revelation through special endowment.

A theory of inspiration involves the concept of what the universe is and how man relates to it. Gnostics looked upon the physical world as evil, and man had to be saved from it. Hence, true knowledge was seen as a supernatural wisdom, as a mystical spiritual enlightenment. In this *gnosis* the believer would come to know the nature of reality. Christ was interpreted as bringing eternal knowledge, but his suffering was only apparent; he could not be limited by his material body.

The Gnostics did not have much to say about the Holy Spirit. Their notions about knowledge and inspiration got in the way. Such matters were not to be examined. Strange ideas and practices concerning the Holy Spirit always get in the way of those who want sound, wholesome experience. People are affected in negative or positive ways by these Gnostic and related notions.

Reactions

Movements such as Montanism and Gnosticism stirred leaders in the Christian faith to take action against them. Their partial conceptions and misconceptions endangered the integrity of the Christian faith. So Christian leaders took action in effecting an organization that could cope with the dangers. This took place quite strongly during the second half of the second century. Three important developments transpired: (1) Administrative organization took shape with the bishops having priority, and with consolidation replacing independent congregations. (2) A collection of scriptural writings became recognized as authoritative. These contained what was considered sound and right. (3) Creeds were formulated. Dr. Walker put it this way: "The church overcame the danger and in so doing developed a closely knit organization and a clearly defined creed, which contrasted with the more spontaneous and charismatic nature of primitive Christianity" (page 51). Heussi, a German writer, observed that about A.D. 50 a person became a member of the church through perceiving baptism and the Holy Spirit and by accepting Jesus as the Lord. In contrast, by the close of the second century one would become a member through acknowledging the creed, the New Testament canon,

185

and the authority of the bishops. (This is somewhat simplified, but it indicates the direction.)

In the field of the Holy Spirit the believer was required to subscribe to the creedal statement about the Spirit and would subscribe to the Church's ritualistic and authorized provisions pertaining to the Holy Ghost. A candidate would be asked, "Do you believe in the Holy Ghost?" And he would reply, "I believe." What he believed and how he believed mattered little. And how and whether he would receive this Spirit was of meager concern. In time questions were not asked; the candidate merely affirmed the given declaration.

Out of these struggles against heresies in their variant forms came action to "defend the faith." Fighting these heresies bore heavily upon the nature of inspiration through the Holy Spirit in beliefs, in practices. Spontaneity received a setback. Dr. Walker wrote this summarizing statement: "Thus...came the Catholic Church with its strong episcopal organization, creedal statement, and authoritative canon" (page 60). The doctrine was officially stated and the sacrament of confirmation and other rites were definitized. Formulated statements and formalized rites fenced in the field. And the Spirit was to come through the authorized priesthood.

No Explanation

During the centuries after Paul's day, little attention was given to interpreting the Holy Spirit, and reception of the Spirit was definitized. Dr. H. B. Swete made this comment in *On the Early History of the*

Doctrine of the Holy Spirit: "In the earliest age of the Church (the Catholic Church) comparatively little attention was paid to the doctrine of the Holy Spirit" (page 5). Leaders stated their belief in the Holy Ghost, but they did not elucidate on what they believed. This trend continued through the centuries.

One reason for this inattention to the Holy Spirit was concern with other matters. A hot controversy over what Arius said about Jesus Christ began about A.D. 320. Arius said that the Father was eternal but that "there was when the Son was not." Such a view was seen by many as being a threat to the entire Christian faith, for it appeared to make the Son "somewhat less." Athanasius championed the view that both the Father and the Son were eternal. While all this argumentation was going on, the Spirit was taken for granted. Little or nothing was said about it.

Another reason for this inattention was the growing concern in church organization and administration. There was fear that church rulership would be developed that would be strong enough to handle differences and disputations and dangers. Church leaders were giving attention to matters that would assure efficiency and power in handling such affairs. Dr. E. F. Scott in *The Spirit in the New Testament* observed that "the ecclesiastical idea" came to have first concern, to dominate Christian thinking. He wrote, "The belief in the Spirit tended to disappear, or to have a merely formal value" (page 125). He went on to say that the Spirit had vital meaning when it "acted directly on men as persons." He added that in later years the Spirit was believed to be receivable only through the Church ordinances. Then the sense of the reality of the Spirit declined.

It is fairly common in times when "the manifestation of the Spirit" wanes to consider expressions of the past quite adequate. This happened in the institutionalized church. As indicated, there came to be three major instruments in the Church for discipline: the canonized Scripture, the authorized creed, and the established episcopacy. Those who rationalized what was happening held (1) that the Spirit had directed the writing of the Scriptures, (2) that the Spirit had directed the formulation of the creeds, and (3) that the Spirit was directing the episcopal leaders of the Church in the use and interpretation of the Scriptures and the creed. This view afforded a sense of authority, of safety, of unity.

E. F. Scott in the previously mentioned writing made this observation: "Belief in the Spirit has its grounds in certain experiences, and in the religion of the later age these had become unusual and to a certain extent unreal" (page 47). On the whole they were assigned to an earlier time as the authoritative foundation for carrying on at a later date. Belief in the Spirit tended to decline in expectation for contemporary authorization.

The Logos Idea

Some theologians used the idea of *Logos* for interpreting the Holy Spirit and other phenomena. From early times the idea of the Logos had grown up among the Greeks. In general it meant the Divine Reason manifested in the universe. The word *logos* was usually translated *word* or *reason*. In the opening chapters of his Gospel John used this idea of Logos to express the divinity of Jesus Christ. Here there is identification with Jesus Christ, who became incarnate and revealed God to man in human terms. This Logos (Word) brought light and life to man. Some identified the Logos as the eternal Spirit of God. Disputation might go on and on. This thinking was in terms of philosophers; it hardly affected the common person. What is written in the Scriptures in this field provides some quotable materials but does little to throw light on the nature of the Holy Spirit for the help of laymen. For large numbers of believers this reference to the Logos did not further clarify the Holy Spirit. Some Christians have asked sincerely, "What is this Logos?"

About Grace

The word "grace" came into prominent usage, and the meaning given it came to accord with the trends in the institutional church. It was thought of as being available through the offices of the Church and transmitted through the sacraments of the established Church. In the following centuries doctrine-makers placed grace to the fore and had less to say about the Holy Spirit. This applies to modern times.

The idea of grace goes back a long way. The basic meaning is well expressed in Joseph's benediction upon his brother Benjamin, "God be gracious unto thee" (Genesis 43:29). The Hebrews, in picturing their God, found it necessary to harmonize qualities they saw in their Jehovah. Sometimes he was described as angry and jealous and exacting. Sometimes he was pictured as gracious and helpful (in the Psalms reference is made to his "loving kindness"). These qualities were not ascribed to the gods of many religions.

Paul emphasized grace. He realized how God had reached out to him—a confused, willful person—when he had been reaching out against God's covenanted disciples. The gracious Christ spoke to him on the road to Damascus, and Paul saw this as expression of God's love. It is obvious why Paul spoke of grace so feelingly: "It is by grace you are saved through faith; it is not of your own doing" (Ephesians 2:4 ff.). Many came to use these quotations from Paul to emphasize grace and faith as the means to salvation.

Paul also had much to say about the inadequacy of works. He was referring to the complex of rules and regulations formulated by priests of "the law." He made contrast between "the works of the law" and the works that would emerge out of "the law of faith" (Romans 3:27). Always he saw "the fruit of the Spirit" coming forth in the life of the person "redeemed by grace" and "saved by faith" (Galatians 5:22, 23). It is imperative that we see the contrast between these two meanings of "works" and use the term accordingly. In the book of James it is used in this nonlegal sense: "Faith without works is dead" (James 2:25, 26). Paul and James indicated how God's grace reaches out in love and how his Spirit brings to pass "works" in the transformed life of the person who responds to divine grace. They set forth how the "works" out of faith were to continue and increase, while the "works" of the law were to be outgrown.

Paul wrote that God in his grace (*xaris*) grants his power (*dunamis*). This power is the Holy Spirit.

Sometimes it looks as if Christians came to speak of grace as his power. These two words ought not to be considered synonymous. Jesus expressed his grace to his men on that last evening, but spiritual power was to come in fullness later. And it did come on the Day of Pentecost. These chosen men were beneficiaries of his grace and recipients of his power.

Grace and the Institutional Church

This dominance of grace came out in the institutional church. Leaders declared that grace was available only through the sacraments conducted by the priesthood. In time this identification developed: "Grace is a supernatural gift of God bestowed on us through the merits of Jesus Christ for our salvation" (*Baltimore Catechism*, Item 109). Grace was not thought of as the Kindness prompting the gift, but as the gift itself. It was considered to be of two kinds: *sanctifying* grace and *actual* grace. The former has been identified as the grace which confers new life of supernatural nature. This enables man to attain the happiness of heaven. Actual grace was also considered supernatural in nature because it enabled man to do good or to avoid evil immediately. This, too, was supposed to be available through the offices of the church. The voice of today's church is definite: "The sacraments do give sanctifying grace" (*Baltimore Catechism*, No. 407). The "Holy Ghost" was assigned to doctrinal statement. Grace was emphasized, not the Holy Spirit as the spiritual power granted by God.

Recently more attention has been given to the Holy Spirit. In a service of confirmation the bishop inquired of the candidates, "Do you believe in the Holy Spirit, the Lord, the giver of life, who came to the apostles at Pentecost and who comes to you today in the sacrament of confirmation?" And the candidates responded, "We do."

Creeds

The five hundred years from A. D. 300 on have been called "the great age of creedmaking." In the strains between ways of thinking there came to the fore the view that there could be one way to believe and that this was to be stated definitely. The interests in those first years were so deep and so widespread that Gregory of Nyassa is credited with saying that if one asked the price of bread the reply might be in terms of doctrine about the Father and the Son. Or one might receive a discourse on the begotten and the unbegotten. Theological disputation was in the air, but it did not include the Holy Spirit.

The first Christian creed on record dates back to about A.D. 200. Although called the "Apostles Creed" it was not written by the apostles. It was so called because Christians thought of it as stating what the apostles believed. In it the Holy Ghost is mentioned two times. The first is to substantiate Christ: "I believe in...Jesus Christ...who was conceived of the Holy Ghost." The major statement affirms, "I believe in the Holy Ghost." There is no interpretation, no clarification. The disciple had merely to affirm.

Debates were waged concerning the Father and the Son. Was the Son as fully divine as the Father? The conflict in the East became a theological battlefield.

192

Those of the Athanasian view took the position that if the Son were less than coeternal with the Father he would not be adequate for insuring the salvation of man. Arius was the chief proponent of the other view. The issue was made to strike close to the average man, even if he could not get hold of the theological arguments. The emperor who had so recently given official sanction to Christianity saw the ineffectiveness of a divided church, so he called the council of Nicea, which met in Asia Minor A.D. 325. Here the "Nicene Creed" was adopted. It affirmed the oneness in substance and the coeternality of the Father and the Son. Anathema was pronounced on those who thought otherwise. Members of the council were not concerned greatly about the Holy Spirit. In the creed they wrote, "We believe in . . . the Holy Spirit"—that was all. The action of this council has been described as the "battle of words," yet it exerted tremendous influence. Creeds of later date were foundationed on it. And this meant that little, if anything, would be said about the Holy Spirit.

A Phrase That Brought Division

For more than two centuries Christian leaders struggled over what is called the *filioque* clause. The fight was direct and heated. The issue was over "the procession of the Spirit." The Eastern Church held that the Holy Spirit "proceeds" from the Father. The Latin (West) Church maintained that the Holy Spirit proceeds "from the Father and the Son." The argument was not concerned with the nature of the Spirit but with the standing of the Son in relation to

193

the Father. The Latin Church made the creedal statement read, "*Sanctus Spiritus qui a Patre* [Father] *Filioque* [and the Son] *procedit.*" This *filioque* clause was first acknowledged in Spain in the Council of Toledo in 589 as a part of the so-called Nicene Creed.

About 857 Photious came to the patriarchate, a man of ability and learning. He affirmed the Nicene Creed without the *filioque* clause. He said that in this matter the Western Church was in heresy. His position was that the Holy Spirit proceeds from the Father through the Son. The pope pronounced an anathema on Photious. There was no healing of the breach. The final break came through the clash between Michael Cerularius, Patriarch of Constantinople, and Pope Leo IX of Rome. The pope called for the patriarch to submit. The patriarch refused. On July 16, 1054, the pope sent representatives to Constantinople for excommunication of Michael Cerularius and all his followers on the high altar of the Church at San Sofia.

The Holy Spirit was set forth as the means for uniting and vitalizing the church. Now disputations about the Holy Spirit broke the church into two hostile groups. In the main, the ministering of the Holy Spirit continued unconsidered.

The churches had unity within the creedal statement affirming belief in the Holy Spirit. The member would say, "I believe." He was not required, not stimulated, not helped to think through what this would mean. The *Baltimore Catechism* sets forth this simple statement: "The Holy Ghost dwells in the Church as the source of life and sanctifies souls through the gift of grace."

Reformation
Creeds
Said Little

Stirring things—the foundations of which had been laid in previous decades—were taking place in the Christian movement at the opening of the sixteenth century. These gave rise to Protestantism in the Lutheran and Reformed branches and to what might be called some "left-wing groups." The church in England changed and took its own course. The Roman Catholic Church made some adjustments and some affirmations that came to be known as the Counter-Reformation. (Writers have used the terms "Protestant Revolt" and "Catholic Revival.") Creeds were formed, and confessions were drawn up. Argument and controversy flourished. Various bodies originated epitomes of belief that came to be considered authoritative. These touched matters of doctrinal concern but were comparatively silent concerning the Holy Spirit. There were some underlying assumptions but few outright affirmations.

Martin Luther

Germany was the area most suited for revolt against the established church. Here the dissatisfactions and unrest of the late Middle Ages reached great heights. There was concern to be free from conventional restraints in both political and church life. (Always there is relationship between what goes on in religion and in the rest of society.)

Martin Luther (1483-1546) was a major factor in the story. His interests and concerns had great influence. Dr. Harold J. Grimm, in *The Reformation Era* (page 98), describes Martin Luther as "endowed with a sensitive conscience, intense emotions, an impetuous temper, a strong will and a powerful intellect"—a remarkable potential for a man trying to find surety in salvation. He celebrated his first mass in May 1507 and throughout it felt completely unworthy. He wondered if his monastic life would be the way to find salvation, and his anxieties increased when he visited Rome a few years later on a mission in the Augustinian order. He was startled by the loose living and low grade of church participation he found there. All this entered into shaping his belief and action.

On returning to Germany Luther applied himself to the study of the Bible, concentrating on the writings of Paul to the Romans and Galatians. Then Johann Tetzel, a Dominican monk, came into the area selling indulgences to procure money for building St. Peter's cathedral in Rome, and Luther rose up in rebellion. He nailed his "ninety-five theses" of protest on the door of the castle church at Wittenburg. This was in October 1517. In 1520 he was excommunicated, and the following year he was placed under the ban of the Empire at the Diet of Worms. During the time he was under this ban he worked out the translation of the Bible, finishing in 1534. This translation, made directly from the Greek text into everyday German, made a new authority available to the people.

Out of his searching and translating came his theological convictions. Foremost was his emphasis on "justification by faith." Concentrating on Romans 1:17 Luther concluded that God forgives sins without man's merits entering into consideration; a believing sinner could be "justified"—that is, he could be freed from guilt of original sin and its consequent penalty. Luther emphasized grace in a new way: he saw it operating not automatically through the sacraments but directly to the individual. He believed that God made this possible by Christ's sacrifice on the cross, and that the Bible (not the priesthood) was the sustaining authority. He affirmed the doctrine of the immediacy of divine grace on the souls of men. His basic emphases were (1) authority of Scriptures, (2) justification by faith, and (3) salvation through grace.

Creeds, Confessions, and Catechisms

Lutheran believers had to identify themselves. Doctrine had to be stated. A new orthodoxy developed. In 1526 the Diet of Speyer decided that since there was no general church council to speak upon matters, each ruler would determine what the religion of his own state should be. This gave some opportunity for the spread of Lutheranism. In 1529 the emperor, during a respite from war, was free to act. Local nobles were apprehensive. Fearing some imperial action contrary to their interest, they filed a protest (thus the word "Protestant" originated). It is possible that some of these nobles were more interested in retaining the church lands they had appropriated than in providing freedom to choose the religion of their area. The existing arrangement had never provided freedom for the individual to choose.

Lutheranism took on new spirit and originality in Bible reading, congregational singing, preaching, and instruction. It stressed the doctrine of "justification by faith" and related matters. On the whole, however, Lutheran theology became settled, definitized. The following were major expressions of Lutheran theology: (1) the Augsburg Confession, read before the Emperor during the Augsburg Diet, June 1530; (2) the Schmalkaldic Articles comprised by Luther himself, the first part of which deals with the conventional fields of Trinity and Christology, June 1536; and (3) the large and small Catechisms issued by Luther in 1529. Against those who tended to be "left-wingers" Luther saw to it that authoritative statements were made. His own popular appeal helped this doctrine to stand.

Orthodoxy About the Holy Spirit

In *Spirit, Son, and Father*, H. P. Dusen sets forth how "it might have been expected that the Protestant revolt of Luther and Calvin . . . would have reclaimed authentic freedom for the Holy Spirit" (page 80), but this did not happen. His Catechism continued the statement: "I believe that it is not of my own reason or by my own strength that I believe in Jesus Christ my Lord; it is the Holy Ghost that by the Gospel has called me, with his gifts enlightened me, through genuine faith has sanctified and sustained me" (Van Dusen, page 81). Then he added that this should be the experience of "all Christendom." Once Luther wrote, "The Holy Ghost writes inwardly in the heart." As time moved on, it became clear that he was thinking of the Holy Spirit's persuading and guiding man through the Scriptures, which he felt had been written under the ministry of the Spirit. He believed that the man who wanted the Holy Spirit would experience it through reading the Scriptures. So came Protestantism's legalism and dogmatism based on the inerrancy of the texts of the Old and the New Testaments. Luther set forth his belief that the Spirit would operate inwardly on the soul of the believer. He never indicated how it would minister except through the sacred writings, which he considered to be the "writing and word of the Holy Spirit."

The Reformed and the Holy Spirit

Two men stand out in the rise of "reformed" Protestantism, Ulrich Zwingli and John Calvin. Zwingli stood out in his native country, Switzerland. In 1523 in the canton of Zurich he established a "reformed" church, holding the Scriptures as his only authority. He saw salvation coming "by grace through faith," not through the priestly church. In this area he agreed with Luther, but the two differed on other points, mainly the Lord's Supper. Unable to get together on these doctrinal matters they went their separate ways. Zwingli died in a religious war between the Roman Catholics and the Reformers. His movement made no significant contribution concerning the Holy Spirit.

John Calvin (1509-1564), the outstanding man in Reformed Protestantism, has been called "the Protestant pope." Credited with bringing in a new authoritarianism, he became its undisputed master after leaving France for Geneva. He built up what might be called a theocracy in which the power resided in him with the church dominating the entire community. Some said that Catholicism was replaced by Calvinism.

Calvin's theology was set forth in his *Institutes of the Christian Religion.* Written in Latin in 1536, these were considered the most systematic creedal exposition of Protestantism. They were systematic; they were severe. His major tenets were (1) the sovereignty of God, eternal, all-powerful; (2) the helpless, fallen condition of man; (3) salvation by election only; (4) baptism as a seal, a sign of grace; (5) heaven and hell as eventual abodes for man; and (6) stern, ethical, practical, disciplined Christian living.

Calvin gave theoretical place to the Holy Spirit and included it in his *Institutes:* "The Holy Spirit is the bond by which Christ efficaciously binds us to himself" (quoted in H. P. Van Dusen's *Spirit, Son, and Father,* page 90). He went on to say that "the Spirit illumines to faith," which is the power to salvation. In Latin he spoke of the *Testimonium spiritus sancti interna,* the inner testimony of the Holy Spirit. For Calvin this functioned through the Scriptures, which he considered thoroughly directed by the Holy Spirit. Faith and grace were his key words in indicating his testimonial experience. He considered his own conversion as a commitment to the sovereign will of God as this was set forth in the Scriptures.

Calvin's influence and power were at their height when Servetus was pronounced guilty of heresy by the Geneva Council and condemned to death by fire in October 1553. To Calvinists, Servetus left the impression that the Son was less than the Father. The Trinitarian doctrine of the Father, the Son, the Spirit had to be maintained and adhered to if there was going to be any salvation for man. The clash was over the Son, not the Spirit (it came in secondarily). Servetus died after crying out, "Jesus, thou Son of the Eternal God." He spoke in contrast to the accepted, "Jesus, Eternal Son of God." The Spirit was taken for granted.

John Calvin affirmed that faith, the source of man's salvation, would be given to the elect by the Holy Spirit through the Word in the austere way his sovereign God would require. And grace was conceived as the condescending expression of this enthroned God. The fervency and friendliness of the Holy Spirit of the Day of Pentecost was not in the written *Institutes* or in the practices that grew out of them. The doctrine of the Spirit as a member of the Trinity was affirmed. That was it!

English Polity

The English broke with the pope on matters of administration of the church. Beliefs about the Spirit continued as before. By 1527 King Henry VIII was wanting a divorce from Catherine of Aragon (of Roman Catholic background). In 1531 he established certain courts which granted him a divorce. Then in 1534 Parliament declared that the king was head of the church in England. It also declared the "Act of Succession" which indicated that Princess Elizabeth, daughter of Henry's second wife Anne Bolyn, was in line of succession. The administrative break with the papacy was almost complete. Henry went even further; he suppressed all monasteries and confiscated their properties. Here his aim was not to reform the church but to obtain funds. He had been using his money in what might be called "loose living" and he was financially embarrassed. Concern about shekels rather than anxiety about spirituality was prompting him. The properties were sold on the market to the highest bidder.

This severance with Rome was an administrative break. No revival, no reformation of religion took place. Following Henry's death in 1547, Edward, son of Jane Seymour, became king. He gave direct attention to church matters, and the spirit of Reformation began to bring changes. The First Prayer Book was adopted. Protestants on the continent were contacted. In 1553 the Forty-nine Articles, stating the theology of the English Church, were published. In nearly all points they state the same belief as the Thirty-nine Articles of 1563, which have remained the authorized statement of the Church of England.

Then Mary (daughter of Catherine, the first wife of Henry VIII) assumed the throne. A rigid Roman

Catholic, she had a dual motivation: to return to the Roman Church and to avenge what she considered the wrongs done to her mother. She set out to destroy the Reformation influence and restore Romanism. Many opponents were sentenced to death. In 1554 England received absolution of the pope and was restored to communion in the Roman Church. The endeavor to restore church lands, however, was unsuccessful. Mary died in 1558—a brokenhearted woman. (The English often referred to her as "bloody Mary.")

Elizabeth came to the throne with her country in a precarious condition. There was war with France. The treasury was empty. Her right to the throne was questioned. The church was in conflict and confusion. Elizabeth worked to bring about better conditions for her people. She chose to be a Protestant; perhaps she had no other choice.

These were the main events of her reign in matters of church: (1) Repeal of what might be called Romanist legislation; (2) affirmation of royal supremacy over the church; (3) restoration of the "Second Prayer Book" of Edward VI with a few alterations; (4) proclamation of the "Act of Uniformity" which required all clergymen to use the "Prayer Book" and all people to attend church; and (5) revision of the Forty-nine Articles of Edward VI into the Thirty-nine Articles (1563) which continued as the creed of the Anglican Church. These were raised to be the law of the land by an act of Parliament in 1571.

Of the Thirty-nine Articles, the first five deal with the Trinity and the person of Christ; the next three with canonical books and creeds; and the largest portion—articles 9-34—with hereditary sin and justification, grace, the church and the sacraments. One section deals with the consecration of bishops and ordination of priests. The articles are rounded out with an affirmation of royal supremacy in the Church of England. This creedal summary is based on things that stood out as major in interest and in importance in those days. The Holy Spirit in nature and function was not in this field of concern.

The same applies to the Book of Common Prayer. It has this to say about the Holy Spirit: "The holy Church throughout all the world doth acknowledge thee; the Father of an infinite Majesty; thine adorable true and only Son; also the Holy Ghost, the Comforter." A choice is given between the Apostles Creed and a more extended one. The former contains this: "I believe in the Holy Ghost," and there is a reference to the conception of Jesus Christ through "the Holy Ghost." The longer statement reads: "I believe in the Holy Ghost, the Lord and Giver of Life, Who proceedeth from the Father and the Son together worshipped and glorified, Who spake by the Prophets." A hymn out of this book expresses the conventional outlook.

> All praise to the Father, the Son
> and Spirit, thrice holy and blessed.
> The eternal, supreme Three-in-One,
> Was, is, and shall be addressed.

Other Religious Movements

A few groups originated in the Reformation period that did not line up with the Lutherans, the Reformists, or the Anglicans. Some spoke out definitely concerning the Holy Spirit. Generally they did not give any interpretations or explanations, but they declared the necessity of this spiritual power and cultivated something about it in their life together. Dr. Van Dusen observed that these groups gave some "recovery of the Scripture's own teaching regarding the Holy Spirit and its operation" (page 82).

Anabaptists. Quite generally this term has been used to identify those who did not believe in infant baptism and objected to Luther's position about baptism. Severe conflict arose. Some opponents of the Anabaptists took extremists in the movement as typical of all Anabaptists, and the term gained ill repute. Generally the movement appealed to those in the humbler strata of society. Anabaptists believed that true Christians should not bear arms and should not hold office. They believed that religious reform should involve social consequences and generally moved toward community living. The congregation was thought of as a community of believers, living together, managing their own affairs. There was to be no control by ecclesiastics. Some have thought that these believers drew their ideal from the congregation of Christians that arose after the Day of Pentecost. They held to a literal adherence to Scriptures, where they found promise of spiritual power and light for the individual. They had inclinations toward the ministering of the Holy Spirit, at times stressing its inward voice. Some thought that this should take precedence over printed words and certainly over the dictates of prelates. Outside opposition and inside factors prompted them toward the more exuberant practices.

Many Anabaptists were persecuted and killed by the "respectables." Stanley Stuber, in *How We Got Our Denominations*, wrote, "Although they were killed in the flesh, their spirit still lived" (page 112).

Quakers. At first the term was used scornfully in England. In 1650 George Fox said that Justice G. Bennett of Derby first called these people Quakers "because we bid him tremble at the word of God." Then the term became popular and was used generally. (The proper name is the *Religious Society of Friends.*)

George Fox (1624-1691) began his stormy ministry in 1647. During the previous year he had experienced a spiritual change that transformed his life. He discounted all external trappings, concluding that Christianity is an experience in which Christ illumines the believing soul; he referred to this as "inner light." He saw revelation not as being confined to the Scriptures (though they were to be received as the word of God) but as enlightening everyone who is a true disciple. He believed that the Spirit of God spoke directly and ministered personally. He taught that this "inner light" would result in a transformed, consecrated life. In a day when revelation was thought of as confined to the Scriptures or to the early church founders, Fox's preaching brought forth marked opposition. Yet his recognition of the need and the possibility for inward spiritual experience held appeal for many. Persecution was marked. During the first decade more than three thousand Quakers, including Fox himself, were imprisoned.

Opposition, persecution, and inner group zeal brought forth extravagances. Some overcultivated the immediate inspiration of the Spirit. Some attributed strange phenomena to the Spirit. This opposition prompted some to leave England and migrate to find a new home in colonial America. Foremost among these was William Penn. The first Quakers to arrive in America—two women—came to the Massachusetts colony in 1658. They were considered witches and were sent back to Barbados, whence they had come. For several years severe laws operated against them and they were treated without mercy. Then came a better day.

The Society of Friends found response in those who were wanting a more spiritual type of Christianity. Many felt that the Reformation had become another orthodoxy. Quakers strongly stressed that "where the Spirit of the Lord is, there is liberty" (II Corinthians 3:17). They continued their emphasis on the availability of "inner light" to all believers, without confinement to any special class or group of "elect." This baptism of the Spirit and close fellowship with the Father were at the heart of their expectation. Rufus Jones, eminent Quaker philosopher, said, "They believe supremely in the nearness of God to the human soul, in direct intercourse and immediate communion, in mystical experience in a firsthand discovery of God." He said this entailed "a reverence for the will of God, wherever it is revealed in past or present, and a high faith that Christ is a living presence and a life-giving energy always within reach of the receptive soul" (Stuber, page 179).

The Catholic Reformation

Pope Paul III cautiously undertook measures of reform. Stimulated by an alarming report on the condition of the church (1538) presented by a committee of cardinals he had appointed because of their interest in reform, he established the Inquisition. He arranged with the emperor for the Council of Trent which was in session for three periods from 1545 to 1563. This council was largely managed by papal legates, and it has been estimated that three-quarters who signed the documents were Italians. Their decrees gave a new statement of tenets for Roman Catholics such as Reformers were getting in their newly formulated statements. Every phase of doctrine attacked by the reformers was redefined. Special attention was given to the whole system of justification, original sin, grace, redemption, the sacraments, the mass, purgatory, and more. Reform measures were enacted. The Council of Trent brought fresh morale, but it said little or nothing in a functional way about the Holy Spirit.

Revivalists
Sought
New Life

This exploration covers several centuries, leading up to the latter part of the eighteenth century and the opening of the nineteenth. It provides a wide look at things. Robert E. Lee is credited with saying, "History teaches us hope." A one-minute squint at the human story will not suffice; it cannot put things together and disclose trends and relationships.

Our inclusive exploration extends from before Pentecost to beyond the present. During these two thousand years we see ups and downs, retreats and advances. We need to get on a prophetic mount of vision where we can see God's way of surveying things.

For now it is advisable to look from the opening of the seventh century into the seventeenth when migrants were crossing the Atlantic to make homes in the New World. At the opening of the seventh century there was a mixed-up western Europe. Well might the pessimist have said that humanity was on its last lap. Some expected that the year 1000 would see the world closing out and Christ returning.

But after the early seventh century much happened that paved the way for worthful developments. These are some of the things of consequence that took place: (1) The extending of notions about the physical universe, going beyond ideas of an earth-centered world; (2) the inventing of the printing press; (3) the reaching out in travel, exploration, migration; (4) the discovering of the Western continent; (5) the experimenting in democratic government; (6) the producing of writings of Renaissance nature. There were many outstanding contributors: Francis of Assisi, Dante, John Huss, Charlemagne, Roger Bacon, Christopher Columbus, and more.

At first glance it might seem that God was taking his time...but he *was* getting somewhere. Sometimes those who thought they were working for God were really getting in the way. When God was wanting to move on, to radiate larger light, these devotees would want to stay put. Through these centuries there was common tendency to assign the Holy Spirit to doctrinal statement or priesthood control, but hunger for that "spiritual something" did not die out. Now and again an individual or a group would act out the desire for spiritual renewal.

In a New Land

A new chapter was written in the story of Christianity with the settling of North America, particularly in the area that came to be known as the United States. To this new country came many of exploratory spirit in religious matters. The high expression of their outlook was set forth in John

Robinson's sermon in Leyden, the Netherlands, when the pilgrims were taking leave to come to the Western land. His text still rings out, "The Lord has yet more light and truth to break forth from his holy word." Some came for adventure, some for gain. Others sought a place where they would be able to worship as they chose. They believed that God would be using them to further his cause. These Pilgrims landed in 1620.

Now it is time to look at the two centuries that followed. Western Europeans came from here and there, bringing a diversity of religions. Anglicans, Lutherans, Reformed, and Roman Catholics represented the established faiths. Then there were the offshoot groups: Quakers, Congregationalists, Methodists. . . and a few Jews. With this diversity the new nation could not have a state church for the whole country. Some colonies started with a colony state church, but this practice gave way. No one group had a sufficient numerical majority. Written into the Constitution of the new nation at the close of the eighteenth century were these statements: "Congress shall make no law respecting an establishment of religion, prohibiting the free exercise thereof," and "No religious test shall ever be required as a qualification to any office or public trust under the United States."

The Methodists

The Methodist movement, started at Oxford University in 1729 by John and Charles Wesley and George Whitefield, stood for repentance and revival.

Its originators stressed "holiness" so much that they and their friends were called the "Holy Club." Because of the way they ordered their living they were dubbed "Methodists." John Wesley's struggle to find himself in right relation with God climaxed in a conversion experience at Aldergate: "I felt my heart strangely warmed. I felt I did trust in Christ, Christ alone for my salvation." He testified that he experienced "an assurance that he had taken away my sins and saved me from the law of sin and death." This experience sent him and his associates out to others, especially the common people. What John Wesley believed about the Holy Spirit is well summarized by John H. Vincent as the creed of Methodism: "I believe that the Holy Spirit is given to all men to enlighten and to incline them to repent of their sins and to believe in the Lord Jesus Christ. . . . I believe that all who are accepted as the children of God may receive the inward assurance of the Holy Spirit to this fact. This is the witness of the Spirit." Here the Holy Spirit is seen as a drawing, warming influence to incline persons to God.

The First Methodist came from England to America in 1760. After a while Francis Asbury was sent over by John Wesley to minister to Methodists in America. They held their first conference in Baltimore in 1784 and their first general conference in 1792. In England the Methodists had gone out to the people preaching God's love, calling to repentance, assuring salvation; they set out to do the same in colonial America. The Holy Spirit was presumed to function in drawing and saving souls. Methodists sang the hymns of Charles Wesley which contained prayers like these: "Breathe,

O breathe thy loving Spirit into every troubled breast," and "Come, Holy Ghost, our hearts inspire!"

During and After the Revolution

Religion was at a low ebb in what was to be the United States during the closing decades of the eighteenth century. In 1789 a group of ministers looked at the new American republic with discouragement. They felt that the people had been falling away from the teaching of their fathers and concluded that "the eternal God has a controversy with this nation." Dr. W. W. Sweet, in *Religion on the American Frontier*, wrote how orthodox believers saw a "melancholy and truly alarming situation" (II, page 55). The East showed decline. The young people were not responding to what they found in church life. There was fear that even the Sabbath might die out.

Colleges were a perplexity to believers. In *The Story of Religion in America* Dr. Sweet relates how in 1782 in Princeton—once a stronghold for training ministers —there were only two "professing Christians" among the students (page 38). Then in 1785 a youth entering Yale found the Bible unpopular with the students; they were reading skeptics and deists. Reports from those times tell of the run-down condition of church buildings and the abandonment of some.

The Revolution had had serious effects. It had taken time, energy, resources, and first place in the interests of many. Connections with the mothering European churches had been severed. Numerous proponents for liberty such as Tom Paine had inclined away from religion. The church had lost place as a ranking influence, and the standing of ministers had gone down. Migrations to the West had taken a toll also. The spirit of criticism of established ways of government and other social institutions had spread to religion. Pioneers who went West were not inclined toward conventionalities. The tax-supported church was gone, and the way of voluntarism had hardly taken hold.

On the Frontier

In *They Gathered at the River* B. A. Weisberger made this general observation: "The frontier was destitute of religion" (page 6). This is a little strong and inclusive, but no one claimed that religion was flourishing. Migrations continued during the latter part of the eighteenth century and the early years of the nineteenth century. First pioneers went to western New York, Kentucky, Tennessee, and the Ohio region. These settlers were busy making a living, and had little time or inclination for building church structures. What they had left back East in church life did not fit where they were. Itinerant preachers who could be at home with the language and facilities of the pioneers were the ones who succeeded. These ministers were not always approved by the church members back East.

The Methodists were growing in numbers in the new land. By 1820 there were approximately a quarter of a million in the United States. Their ministers were largely self-educated, and their meetings showed considerable spontaneity. The Methodists adjusted fairly well to frontier ways, but in the "cultured" East they did not rate high. The Baptists had a similar story.

This increase in Methodists and Baptists did not always please conventional church leaders. Some of the churches in the East raised money and sent out missionaries to frontier settlers. Occasionally the term "heathen" was used in reference to the frontiersmen.

Revivalism

The revival at the opening of the nineteenth century in the young United States had a frontier setting and atmosphere. A little earlier the "Great Awakening" had taken place in the colonies. This had followed prevailing patterns of theology, with more intensified preaching. Camp meetings became popular. Revivalism was in its heyday from about 1798 through 1820. Weisberger opined, "By 1830 the genuinely frenzied and spontaneous revival was largely a memory" (page 21). In some places, chiefly in the South and in mountain areas, the revival continued. Weisberger referred to this revivalistic expression as a "binge of unharnessed emotionalism," but proponents saw it as "an outpouring of the Spirit."

Revival meetings involved mass participation, but the concern was with the individual. The aim was to save souls, and the person himself had to experience being saved. Each man or woman was to have a change of heart which would take place suddenly and publicly under strong emotional pressure. Sometimes this pressure was excruciating. Heaven and hell were pictured graphically as preachers pushed seekers to want to be saved.

Back of all these revival endeavors was the theology that man is sinful by nature and because of Adam's fall deserves damnation forever. The revivalists preached, too, that the death of Christ made atonement for the sins of man through God's grace. They stressed human depravity, the horrors of hell, and the glories of heaven. Weisberger (page 27) described the process with this general picture: "First a man [or woman] felt a gnawing sense of guilt and wickedness, and then a frightening awareness that hell was an entirely just punishment for such a wretch." The sinner, "stripped of pride and self esteem, was ready to throw himself on God's mercy." Revival preachers set before the sinners the expectation that there would come some "climactic emotional experience" that would assure salvation. This conversion was viewed as a supernatural happening. The expectation was set up that there should be a mighty baptism of the Holy Ghost.

Physical expression in this baptism of the Holy Ghost was anticipated. Sometimes persons would fall prostrate on the ground, crying aloud their agonies and distress. Many experienced various manifestations, such as the "jerks"—a spasmodic twitching of the body. Generally this took place in meetings, but it might also happen when a person was alone. In contrast, some would lie motionless. There was the case of Rachel Martin in Kentucky who was credited with not moving for nine days before she obtained the desired "blessed assurance." W. W. Sweet refers to a case recorded in the journal of Benjamin Lakin, an itinerant minister. In 1802 a young woman lay in such immobility and Lakin commented: "Surely it is the

Lord's doings and it is marvelous in our eyes" (*Religion on the American Frontier*, IV, page 223). There might be dancing, laughing, singing, rolling, barking, and jumping as well as jerking or having the "silent possession" by the Spirit. Noise and excitement and bodily expression were generally associated with salvation through the Holy Ghost.

Without Ethical Change

Often there was little if any relationship between what happened in the camp meeting and the converts' pattern of ethical living. On the whole, salvation was looked upon as coming through the grace of God, not through the works of man. Many would come to a camp meeting with little or no concern about being saved. Sometimes individuals or families would drive many miles and camp for days or weeks.

On the frontier a revival was the social event of the year. Those not religiously inclined often brought along whiskey for the outing. The intensity of the "spiritual experience" tended to merge persons together and usual restraints might diminish. This applied to sexual restrictions also. Camp meeting skeptics were credited with saying that "more souls were begot than saved." As time went on, those in charge of the camp meetings sought to weed out any who came without good intent.

Revivalists' Conception of the Holy Ghost

People who attended camp meetings were highly concerned about getting the Holy Ghost. They made much of what Paul wrote in Hebrews 4:2 about the necessity for "faith in the hearers." They stressed how the word should be "quick and powerful." Preachers believed that they should make it so in order to convince persons of their sin. They took Paul's statement quite literally:

For the word of God is quick and powerful, and sharper than any two-edged sword, piercing even to the dividing asunder of body and spirit, and of the joints and marrow, and is a discerner of the thoughts and intents of the heart. —Hebrews 4:12.

Preaching by the Spirit was to be piercing and penetrating. The "intellectual" sermon did not rate well. In the minds of the campers it left "the heart without interest and the conscience without alarm." Little was said about guiding into "all truth." The largeness of God was not emphasized. The Spirit was to focus on the immediate contact of God on the soul so as to impel sinners to repentance. Intensity rather than insight was emphasized.

Some people associate the Spirit of God with meditation and contemplation. These would think of of him as speaking in the quiet. Marxist critics of religion have identified religion as the opiate of the people. This "opium" would keep them quiet in the present, while they dreamed of glorious times to come in the hereafter. Revivalists thought of the glories, the beauties of heaven, but there was no comtemplative silence about their dreaming. It was something to be sung and shouted about. Rather than an opiate it served as adrenaline, and they went into action during their meetings, not afterward.

Schisms over the Spirit

Most of the orthodox churches did not have much to say about the Holy Spirit. It was designated and sanctioned in the Apostles Creed but did not enter into teaching or preaching to any great degree. By and large, when mentioned, the Spirit was referred to as the instrument of grace. Many churchmen, particularly those in the East, denounced the Spirit-fired meetings of the revivalists. In the Presbyterian Church two parties emerged—the "Old Side" (endorsing the former theology way of study, and type of meetings) and the "New Side" (endorsing spiritual emphasis). In one section of Kentucky a new presbytery was set up in 1801; these Presbyterians were ardent revivalists. Their ministers, with no seminary training, taught themselves to exhort. Conservatives branded them illiterates. These "Cumberland Presbyterians," who wanted the fervor of the Spirit, remained a separate body until 1906. Their view was that a convert instinctively did what was right at the urging of the Spirit, not because of the dictate of a creed.

Occasionally differences would show up in revival meetings. Some people would advocate ultimate expression as the Spirit prompted. Others would advocate more restraint. It irked a preacher like James McGready to have anyone dampen the Spirit. After he had exhorted a man halfway to salvation and expected that the man soon would receive the baptism of the Spirit, he became angry when someone held a bottle of camphor under the penitent's nose to revive him.

Revivals and Righteousness

Some insisted on relating the ministry of the Holy Spirit with righteous living. A foremost advocate of this was Lyman Beecher (1775-1863) who, while in Yale, came to know President Timothy Dwight quite well. In later life he told how he learned from President Dwight that in ministry the greatest thing was not theology or controversy but concern "to save the souls of men." Of his own conversion he once said, "The Lord drove me, but I was ready." It was said that he was overendowed with "the Yankee urge to work." He was a fighter for a cause, and his two chief targets were infidels and Unitarians. Lyman Beecher was a revivalist who connected righteousness and revival. He said that God governed the universe by a moral system and that good moral living was an essential part of salvation. He applied this to government as well as everyday living. He saw the Holy Spirit as indispensable in the work of redemption and preached that the Spirit would be aided if men would behave in a way approved by God even before they were regenerated. He went to the Bible for proof. This did not square with the preaching of revivalists who held that man was incapable of goodness through his own powers and could not be expected to live righteously before he was regenerated. Some thought that Beecher was getting dangerously near to the freedom of will, which was regarded as heretical. What he was saying was that man carries both responsibility and ability and should use these in developing qualitative living personally and in his society—with God as his ally. For Lyman Beecher a revival was to have continuing influence and enthusiasm directed toward building a moral society. This would provide a better foundation for regeneration.

Overview of Revival Days

The "revival flourish" before and after the opening of the nineteenth century came out of several reactions and interactions of the times. A new day needed a new spiritual life. Many had come to feel that conventional church life was stiff and stale. The pioneers were not disposed to have churchmen of the East impose cultured ways on them. These frontier critics felt that religion needed a blood transfusion. They responded to the stimulations of their Western life. These were some of the major factors: (1) Frontiersmen were individualistic; they did not want to be dominated. The religion they wanted had to touch the individual person. (2) They wanted a friendly community in their religion. The social aspects of camp meetings appealed. In the revivals the group helped the person to sense individual salvation. (3) They wanted exhilaration and excitement. (4) They wanted something they could be sure about in a not-too-long period of time. They wanted to know that they were saved—instantly. What they called the Holy Ghost offorded these experiences. Their "spiritual baptism" brought on in the revival setting was moving, warming, soul-stirring, and immediate.

They lacked background for identifying what the Holy Spirit was to be and how it was to affect lives. Many felt that if they made such exploration, it would show lack of faith and get in the way of the coming of the Spirit. Their understandings and desires were immediate and narrow. They went to the Bible and found passages that harmonized with their conceptions of what ought to happen when a person received the Holy Spirit. The opposition of others confirmed their assumption that they were endowed by the Spirit. Cynics and doubters would not appreciate or understand what they said about their experiences.

These revivalists sought vitality in religious experience, but they needed foundation for and function in spiritual living. Without this the emotional glow would be short-lived. There was need for continuing ministry.

Inquiries
For Our
Exploration

CONSIDERATION ONE

1. What is the difference between the person who explores and the person who "just looks around to see what can be seen"?
2. How do you respond to the comment, "I don't need to inquire. I've had the Spirit"?
3. How do you respond to the testimonial comment, "I've had the Spirit. That's enough"?
4. Through the centuries why has so little been said in interpreting the Holy Spirit? What factors have made for silence or for "official quotings"?
5. What has prompted many moderns to give low rating to "the Spirit"?
6. What happens when we place something such as the Holy Spirit in the realm of the supernatural, outside human consideration?
7. In a definition or a designation of something we generally set to the fore some classification term and then expand our identification. Thus, "Geranium is a flowering plant...." What word would you use next in this identifying sentence, "The Holy Spirit is..."?

8. What does "the laboratory of living" mean to you in relation to studying the Holy Spirit?
9. How does the emphasis on experiencing the Holy Spirit by some contemporary religious groups complicate our situation yet require exploration of the Holy Spirit?
10. How would you converse with a theology-minded person who says, "The Spirit is the presence of God ministering in man"?
11. What do you see appropriate in the Greek word *dynamis* that was used to denote the Holy Spirit? How would you use it to denote the Holy Spirit?
12. What expectancies should we set up about "confirmation" for "receiving the Holy Spirit"? What is the person to expect? How do you indicate to a child what to expect? To an adult?
13. When you were coming into the church by baptism, what were you taught about the Holy Spirit? Was the Holy Spirit explained so you could understand?
14. A brother of the Orient commented that when he asked members of the Church about the Holy Spirit, all they gave him was quotations from the Bible which did not have meaning for him. How would you interpret the Spirit to a person with Orient background?
15. An Indian of North America stood by a tree sacred to his people. We stood together in silence. He spoke of Wakonda, a designative name for the Great Spirit among his people. How would we converse with him about the Holy Spirit?
16. What are situations in today's world of religion that call us to have clear interpretation of the Holy Spirit?
17. How is this interpretation, this experience of the Holy Spirit, needed in our own church today? Make this an exploration rather than a denunciation or a validation. What do we need to see and do that we may experience spiritual vitality?

CONSIDERATION TWO

1. What qualities and capacities does a person have that distinguish him from a robot?
2. How is creating man as a person a great expression of faith on God's part?
3. How may a person be strong on "charm" and weak on "choice"?
4. How is becoming a person an inter-persons experience?
5. What is the fallacy in the statement, "I am a self-made man"? What are some things that this man received from others, from society?
6. What is unsound in this statement, "I never made myself—others did"? When a person is dominated by others, what are some things that are of his own choosing?
7. What qualities in persons do you consider conducive to developing "abundant personhood" in other persons? What kind of "managing" is helpful?
8. What and how is self-evaluation healthy and when is it otherwise? What if there is no self-evaluation? What kind of self-evaluation would get in the way?
9. What happens in the person who "settles down"? How is the opposite likely to prove unhealthy?
10. How shall we work on the question, "Who am I?" How can working on this provide sound, worthful experience? How can it distort the person? What resources may we as persons, as families, as church provide for this inquiring?
11. What would happen in persons if God were to answer all their inquiries with specific answers and detailed solutions? After ten years what would be the condition of the inquiring person?
12. What would happen to humans as persons if God were

to intervene and set things right apart from any human endeavor? What attitude might develop in persons with respect to responsibility and consequences?

13. How may living with nature enrich or impoverish, release or restrict persons in their total personhood? It is said that some persons live with nature and explore nature while others live off nature and exploit nature. What difference does this make in the persons' goals and values? What do you see as God's role in nature?

14. What kind of society will be most contributive to the development of persons of "abundant" nature? What resources can a "good" society contribute to the development of persons of "abundant" quality?

15. How does social stratification affect the personhoods of those who live in a stratified society? Contrast the influences in the several strata.

16. What do salesmen and propagandists mean when they say that a certain popular product has "personality"? What do they have in mind when they say their product will "give so much" to the "personality" of users? How is this a misconception of what "personality" is? (Every person has personality whether it is appealing or not.)

17. What kind of family living is good resource for developing persons with wholesome personhood?

18. How may a church or a person have right or unsound conceptions of persons as foremost? What constitutes a sound conception of persons as most worthful?

19. How may a society, a church rate other things ahead of persons in their scales of what is most worthful?

20. How do you see the Holy Spirit as resource for developing persons with "abundant" quality?

CONSIDERATION THREE

1. If a youth of eighteen were to leave his family, his community, and go off alone on "an isolated island," how would he not be an "atomistic" person?
2. How does the person have relationship with those who have lived prior to his time? When and how is this good and when and how is this not to the good? What person-building resources may one get from persons who have lived in former times?
3. In our modern world is it possible for a person to go apart and live by himself?
4. What were the standards and values of Willie Loman for personal development? What were the shortcomings in his social relationships?
5. Contrast the intent to "improve personality" as set forth by "charm schools" and by publicists for products with the intent to "improve" the total personhood. Contrast the focusing on externals with emphasis on developing inner "spiritual qualities." What is the rightful emphasis on the externals?
6. The sage of the Hebrews said, "A merry heart makes a cheerful countenance" (Proverbs 15:13). Contrast putting on a facial act and reflecting in the face what is in the person. What is the essence of true merriment?
7. Some commentators consider that modern youth are quite "discerning." This means that they can detect what is "phony." This refers to those who put on an act of being friendly. These youth often say that they can detect the person whose face is genuine, whose handshake is real, whose voice quality speaks the truth. What did one youth mean when he said that he wanted to be received and considered as a real person

and "not as a statistic, not as a number"? How is genuineness basic in true relationship?

8. How are we going to relate the worth of one person to the worth of others? Illustrate how in church life we may overemphasize the one specific person and neglect others. What happens when we elevate one person and overlook the worth of another person?

9. What do we set up as criteria for measuring the worth of a person? Are we using the standards of contemporary society? To what degree are these valid?

10. Illustrate what is meant by chain reaction in the large story of human relationships. Give instances of desirable and undesirable chain reactions. What have been some influences in your life that came indirectly in chain reaction?

11. How is language expression more than verbal expression? Illustrate how the whole person speaks. How does this require the person to "hang together"? How have some persons spoken to you through more than words?

12. To what extent do we speak with God in language that expresses our total personhood? Do we express ourselves to God or do we take the easy, immature way and say, "He understands"? How do we need to be clear and honest in speaking out to God? How does this clarity and honesty help us develop spiritually?

13. How may a person get so concerned about how he expresses himself that he gets in the way of vital conversation? How does this apply to talking to God, with God?

14. To what extent and in what way is it advisable to "open up" and reveal what is "in the inside of us"? With what persons may this be done? When is this advisable? What is a healthy way of doing this with God?

15. How is the person who ministers to persons of lower level in personal qualities going to "keep up" so he will be in good condition, with wholesome personhood, and be able to keep on ministering to these persons?
16. What are we going to have in mind when we say that persons are worth more than anything else? What will happen if we put high worth on some persons as they now are? What is it in persons that we are going to prize?
17. What tremendous responsibility is placed on parents, on a congregation, on a community when we sense that a babe comes as a candidate to become a person? And what call to happy, creative stewardship is involved?
18. Contrast gregarious getting together with consociation that gets us on the way.
19. How are we going to interpret and experience the Holy Spirit as resource for enabling wholesome personal relations with other persons, with God?

CONSIDERATION FOUR

1. How may we see and interpret living as a continuing experiment in the laboratory of life? What characterizes good experimenting? What would be a contrasting view?
2. How did Alma make living with faith an experimental experience? (See Alma 16:151.)
3. What is the connotation in the word *resource* in its denoting something that is not used up? What

continuing quality should there be in real resources?

4. How would it be unfair for God to require a person to achieve a quality of living without God's providing resources for achieving this quality of living?

5. Give instances of persons living in the midst of available resources without their knowing that these resources were there.

6. Contrast the person who wants God to provide resources, ready-made, right now, with the person who expects to work with God, tapping resources over a longer period of time.

7. Give illustrations of misusing physical resources, of exploiting them for purposes not lined up with God's purposes. What have been the motivations for using these resources? Why was the use shortsighted?

8. How may mental resources be misused? What constitutes sound use of mental resources?

9. How may persons misuse spiritual resources for ends that do not accord with God's plan and purpose? What is worthy motivation for wanting spiritual resources?

10. What do you set forth as examples of "existing," with little of worthful living involved in this "existing"? Illustrate how some conditions of living take the time and energy of persons, of families for merely keeping alive.

11. How may a so-called "spiritual" person become narrowed and set up partial pictures of what constitutes "abundant living"? How would such persons have a restricted picture of the "spiritual resources" they want?

12. What can happen when an immature person gets hold of big-power resources?

13. Illustrate how we can contaminate resources and undermine possibilities for good living. Apply this to physical, mental, social, spiritual resources. Set forth the healthy use of these resources.

14. What happens when a person concentrates on physical resources and leaves out the spiritual resources?
15. How may it be advisable for God to hold back granting some resources to some persons and to some groups?
16. Contrast prayers beseeching God for right-now, ready-to-go resources with prayers seeking guidance in developing resources, in finding resources, in using resources.
17. How would you go about getting resources for going to Orissa, India, for missionary ministry? What would be some contrasting views about getting these resources?
18. What would happen if God put dollar bills on money trees for the Saints?

CONSIDERATION FIVE

1. Illustrate how a resource good for one thing may get in the way in another field.
2. A youth, on hearing the story of creation as narrated in Genesis, and the pronunciamento of God, "It is good!" observed, "In fairness to God, we ought to ask, 'Good for what?' " How is it advisable that we ask this question?
3. Identify some tabus that get in the way of effective exploring of God's resources.
4. Give instances of building up God's resource in the physical world. Give instances in which man has brought deterioration in God's provided resources. Apply to the soil, to the atmosphere, to bodies of water. Apply to our physical bodies.

5. Do we think of God's resources as a storehouse of static resources or as a treasury of ever-in-action resources? What difference does this make? Do you think of anything that God provides as static?

6. How may recent explorations in the field of human reproduction become asset or liability in the bank of God's resources? How might we produce animals rather than persons? How might we produce persons of higher quality?

7. May excursions into outer space open hitherto unseen resources to men on earth? May we find out something about radiation that would make a difference? What shall we do with our findings?

8. Moderns are beginning to sense the membership of our Earth as a small planet in a universe with untold number of galaxies, billions of stars, planets, asteroids, and other celestial objects of varying sizes, shapes, and characteristics. How do we include these in our bank of resources? How do we appreciate the sun with its effective temperature of about 10,000 degrees F. giving its energy to our Earth's surface of 1.94 calories per minute per square centimeter? Do we see other members of our universe as resources? And how?

9. How do we see the elements in our universe as resources? Do we see these elements as static or as ever in process? For instance, how are we learning to use uranium? For constructive or for destructive purpose?

10. How are we viewing speed and potentials for speed in our universe? What is our reaction to the speed of our planet Earth, 18.5 miles per second? What is our reaction to the requirement of 7.0 miles per second as escape velocity for getting away from the pull of our planet? How do we see this speed functioning in keeping us in orbit in relation to the rest of the universe?

11. What are the resources of our troposphere, that layer region of the atmosphere which is in contact with the earth's surface, located between ground level and six miles up at the poles and thirteen miles at the equator? How do we see this as God-provided resource?

12. How has man explored in the field of radio waves and other waves for the transmission of sounds? What resources does the universe offer in this field? How have we explored and used these potentials? How have these developments been affecting human life? To the good? To the not-so-good? What do you see lying ahead?

13. How do you see man as a steward in respect to a world bank of resources? How do you see man responsible for using these resources for abundant living?

14. What would happen if God were to "open the bank" and give every person in your congregation a million dollars? What would be the reaction? How does receiving call for understanding?

15. Contrast God's charging us for use of these resources with God's wanting us to share in the responsibilities of managing. How do we "get with" God in this?

16. What are effects on man, on God's work, when persons affirm that salvation is free and does not cost them anything?

17. Do you see man backward in exploring spiritual resources? Or would you say that man has been offward? (He got off the track.)

18. What do you see as sound conception of God's bank of resources? How you see man as entitled or not entitled to draw on these resources, including the spiritual resources?

19. When it is said that we need an Einstein in spiritual

matters, what are seen as needs, as possibilities? How can the Restoration Church function in this field?

CONSIDERATION SIX

1. What is unsound in this man's comment, "What is really real, I can get my hands on"? He meant that reality is always manually tangible.
2. What is real in a person? Not his body organism. Not in what can be touched, smelled, heard in this physiological body. The essence of this person's personhood is in his thinking, in his evaluating, in his identifying and so on. How do we sense the reality of a person's personhood?
3. How has man's division of reality into two contrasting and sometimes opposing fields of reality complicated and confused our notions as to what is real? How did two different ways of getting next to these two fields of reality develop, one for the material and one for the spiritual? How general is the notion today that the material is either inferior or not good at all?
4. What reality do you see those omit who insist that nothing evil exists?
5. In the identification of evil as getting out of alignment with God in purpose, in process, in personal relations, how inclusive do you see evil to be? And what is the way of deliverance from evil? Would there be some one "quickie" experience for turning evil to good?
6. In the conception that good is lining up with God in all ways, in right alignment with all God's realities,

how does this right living with God involve getting with available resources?

7. How may it be said that the person who disregards or denies spiritual realities lives partially?

8. How are some ways that a person or a group or a church may misconceive and misconnect with spiritual reality and come out weak or wrong?

9. How can we misinterpret the nature of God and build up relations with a Somebody other than the God who is? How would you have personal relations with a God whom you conceive as a stern judge, as a finalized lawgiver, as a father with favorites, as a chief wanting adoration and praise and gifts, as a bargain driver?

10. How does the notion that if a person says "Jesus" he will clear everything with God at the instant hardly square with the conception of spiritual reality that functions in purpose, in process God's way?

11. Do you vision God's operating as a gigantic business with specialists so that we turn to the department of farming, the department of athletics, or the department of romance if we have a special interest? Do you see God operating with compartmentalization?

12. What are the implications of thinking of personhood as "an emerging process"? How long does the person plan to have creative connection and consociation with God in the business of living as a person?

13. What would you say to the boy who wondered if there was anything "out there" that would help him to grow up as the sun helps the plant to grow? Could you compare God's life-giving forces for helping man to the life-giving forces in the sun that help the plant to grow?

14. Interpret and apply the comment of the man who said that there must be some power in the universe that produces persons because he is a person and he comes

out of the universe. Do you see the universe having person-producing forces?

15. What kind of experience with spiritual reality would be meaningful and convincing to others to cultivate assurance that there is spiritual reality? How would you guide a person and coordinate with a person in making contact with spiritual reality? How would you speak his language, language that speaks today?

16. Contrast the view that God is love with the functional view of getting with God in projects that entail God and express love to other persons.

17. What is your response to the person who says, "Tell me how the Holy Spirit works"?

CONSIDERATION SEVEN

1. What has been your idea of "natural man"? Did this picture God's man as thoroughly evil, as incapable of goodness? Do you consider that God put evil desires and drives in man?

2. Translators use the available words that are the most meaningful, that carry the meanings and moods of the day. How, then, is it essential that we seek to discover what the writer and the translator were trying to say? How does this apply to the use of the word "natural"?

3. What is your picture of the "natural man" that God designed and designs? God set out to create man as person. This involves capacity for choosing. What, then, might this man, with capacity and inclination for

choosing, do with the powers that God placed and places in man?

4. What is your reaction toward this comment: "I want God to give me the Holy Spirit and then I won't have to do any choosing"? What would this kind of functioning of the Holy Spirit do to man as person?

5. What difference does it make whether we hold to the view of supernatural or to the view that there are natural things that we do not yet understand, but which are understandable?

6. When man has experience of revelation through the ministry of the Holy Spirit does he think with his own intellectual and emotional powers or are they "turned off"?

7. How may we make a conclusion about happenings in nature and state something as natural law, when our experience and thinking are inadequate for making such general conclusions? Illustrate how this applies to religious experience.

8. A wise man has said, "We need to be careful about what we set forth as 'celestial law.' We can be premature and immature in our conclusions." What was he meaning? What kinds of conclusions about God and his workings may we make without adequate data and insight? The wise saint who made the foregoing affirmation was referring to two things in particular: the workings of the universe and the hereafter.

9. Did Alma mean that "the state of happiness" was the state designed by God for man (Alma 19:75)? If so, would not this state be the natural state for man? How does man lose this "happy living" when he gets away from God?

10. How does the use of the word "natural" differ today from its use two thousand years ago when the New Testament was written and from an earlier period

when Alma and Benjamin spoke? How do our notions of the ways of nature keep developing?

11. What difference does it make whether we think of God as having finished creation or as continuing to create? How does this apply to our interpreting and expecting the ministering of the Holy Spirit today?

12. When we think of "the laws of God" do we think of these laws as prescriptive or as descriptive? What difference does this make in our relating to and working with God? In interpreting and experiencing the Holy Spirit?

13. In terms of natural law what do you give as identification of *miracle?* Give illustrations of things in natural phenomena in the physical world once thought of as supernatural or miraculous that we now interpret as natural. Do you see this development continuing?

14. In the fields of natural phenomena with which we are conversant, we note that we have to comply with requirements for contact and operation—an example, the conduct of electricity. Do you see this applying to the Holy Spirit as natural process?

15. Name some phenomena formerly considered outside the natural that are now considered natural. Do you see something of this nature taking place in the realm of the Holy Spirit? Are there some aspects of the ministry of the Holy Spirit that we are understanding more?

16. How may we be inclined to definitize about the Holy Spirit and state regulations and "laws" when we do not have the background of experience for doing so?

17. In what functionings do you see the Holy Spirit as natural resource? What requirements do you see for experiencing this resource—requirements functional rather than prescriptive?

18. What in your opinion does a person miss who does not experience the ministering of the Holy Spirit?

CONSIDERATION EIGHT

1. How do you see Jesus planning his daily living so he could keep up and keep going on? What did he do to "keep his batteries charged"?
2. How did Jesus go about building up resources in his men and getting them to have contact with available spiritual resources?
3. What guidelines do you get on developing youth from the story of the twelve-year-old Jesus in the temple? What interests in living had he been developing? What resources had he been developing?
4. How do you picture Jesus conversing with the doctors in the Temple? What do you think he was seeking to do? How would you converse with a twelve-year-old?
5. What significance do you see in the fact that the "temptation" followed the water and Spirit baptism of Jesus? How did this require that Jesus understand what spiritual power is for?
6. Some say that Jesus' remark that he had "other food" carries the implication that Jesus did not need to indulge in eating material food. How does this view not square with Jesus' inclusive program of living? How did he use meal-eating as part of his program with his men?
7. How did Jesus' comment that his food came as he did what his Father wanted him to do set forth the role of "spiritual exercising" in relation to "spiritual food receiving"?
8. What in your opinion did Jesus want to happen in the three men he took with him to the Mount of Transfiguration? How did he want this resource experience to affect them? What was his counsel about telling others of this experience? What are your pointers about "telling testimonies"?

9. This "bottom" experience of Jesus on the cross has bothered many. How was this an essential part of Jesus' total man-God experience? What does it reveal about the place of resources in one's life? What kept Jesus from getting embittered?

10. What do you think radiated from Jesus so that one of the thieves turned to him in confession and confidence? How was this one of the high points in Jesus' life?

11. What kind of resources for power and expressions of power would the conventional Jew have expected of a Messiah? What would have been the outcome if Jesus had used power in their way?

12. Do you consider that those close to Jesus believed that he had enough resources at his command to liberate himself and put down his opponents? What would have happened to his cause if he had done so? What constitutes moral utilization of resources?

13. How would it have been advisable or inadvisable for Jesus to go show himself to Pilate and to the high priest and thereby validate himself? What might have been their reaction? What would have been their bases for seeing him as Messiah?

14. How would you identify Jesus Christ as a person today through his personhood, without use of conventional clothing and the like? How would you identify him as the Christ?

15. Why did Jesus advise so often, "fear not!" What constitutes wholesome confidence? What are its roots and resources?

16. What are some experiences in the life of Jesus that stand out as revelations of extra endowment of spiritual power?

1. How do you characterize a laboratory school? How would this differ from a catechetical school? From a "chapter-and-verse" school?
2. How might Jesus be considered as carrying on a laboratory school with his chosen men? What was he planning to have his men find out? What laboratory experiences did he arrange for them to have?
3. How did Jesus' twelve men constitute a company of twelve persons with wide differences in their general personhoods, their relationships with others? What held these men together in their laboratory school? What would hold them together after Jesus would leave them?
4. How was the person-with-person relationship so essential in this school of twelve apostles? How was this going to be essential in their future work? How was there two-way communication?
5. Picture a company of twelve persons working together today in a laboratory school in spiritual projects. Indicate differences between persons. What would hold them together and afford cooperation and fellowship?
6. How were conversation circles an essential part of the school of the twelve? What were some of the concerns of these men that called forth comment from Jesus? How did some concerns and viewpoints indicate problems that Jesus faced in training his men? How did some of their questions and comments indicate their spiritual immaturity?
7. What kind of testifying did Jesus encourage? What topics, what viewpoints did Jesus counsel against using? What distinguishes testifying from "selling" and propagandizing? What in a person has to back up his testifying?

8. How do you explain that Jesus said little about the Holy Spirit during these years with his men? How do you think he was laying a foundation for his consideration of the Spirit during his closing days?

9. How might the Holy Spirit have been misinterpreted by these men? How do some "intimate" groups misinterpret the Holy Spirit today? How do you think Jesus would teach them about the Spirit today?

10. Interpret and apply this truism, "That which has large potential for goodness has large potential for misuse." How does this apply to potentials in a person? How does this apply to the Holy Spirit?

11. After the seventy had been out in laboratory ministry, they returned to report on what had taken place. Luke reported this about Jesus' reaction: "In the same hour he rejoiced in the Holy Spirit." About what was Jesus rejoicing?

12. How does Jesus' affirmation in Nazareth indicate what he wanted his men to see and do? Jesus began with the affirmation, "The Spirit of the Lord is upon me" (Luke 4:18). How does Jesus' comment set forth what he anticipated would be the functioning of the Spirit in his men in their ministry?

13. What is the significance in Jesus' use of the word "teach" in his counsel to his disciples: "The Holy Spirit will teach you in that very hour what you ought to say" (Luke 12:12)? How would some other word have changed the meaning of the functioning of the Spirit? How does the phrase "in that very hour" require some relating to the inclusive experience with the Holy Spirit? How may this phrase be soundly and unsoundly interpreted and applied?

14. How is it significant that in the transfiguration experience (Matthew 17) the counsel was "Listen to him!" rather than "Look at him!"?

242

15. In Matthew 12:28 how did Jesus make the Holy Spirit a forceful dynamic power whose functioning is to bring to pass good against evil opposition? What was Jesus wanting his men to see about the vigorous quality of his cause, the vital functioning of the Holy Spirit?
16. In Jesus' laboratory school how might we say that at his departing there was a genuine "commencement day" in the sense that the real commencing was now to start?

CONSIDERATION TEN

1. How was the Last Supper an appropriate setting for Jesus to bring to his men the promise of the coming of the Holy Spirit? What did he do with his men that laid foundation for the conversation about the Holy Spirit?
2. How did his affirmation of their relationship as friends contribute to this setting? How would the relationship of friendship differ from that of servantship in associating with Christ Jesus? Is there place for both relationships?
3. The Jews used their word *ruah*, meaning *breath*, to denote the Spirit of God. They would refer to "the breath of life" as given by God. To what degree would this conception be adequate or inadequate for designating what Jesus had in mind as the Holy Spirit?
4. How does Jesus' way of teaching throw light on the teaching ministering of the Holy Spirit? How would catechetical teaching and dogmatic teaching not fit into this picture? What was Jesus aiming to do in his teaching?
5. What implications are involved in Jesus' statement to his

men that he had many things to say to them but they were not ready to "bear" them at that time? What does this indicate about the longer-time program of inspired teaching? How does this reveal that God is conditioned by our condition?

6. How has the common conception of "comfort" as sympathy and the like weakened the conception of the Holy Spirit as "Comforter"? How does the conception of "Strengthener" give a stronger, more functioning conception of the Holy Spirit?

7. What is the significance of Jesus' using the term *agape* to designate the quality of love he had in mind? How was the Greek language well equipped to indicate the quality of love he had in mind? How are many modern languages inadequately equipped so that "love can mean almost anything"? What did Jesus mean by love? What qualities inhere in *agape?*

8. How may "bringing to remembrance" help or hinder? How did Jesus mean that the Holy Spirit was to minister in remembering? How does what we choose to remember constitute a criterion of our spirituality? In what way is the *how* of remembering important along with the *what* of remembering?

9. What do you see Jesus had in mind as healthy testimony? How was he building up experience for testimony in his men? What kind of testimony did he discourage? What kind of testimony did he encourage?

10. How was Jesus implying to his men that thereafter the Holy Spirit would be functioning in their testifying as he had been functioning?

11. What was disclosed during the Last Supper about the disciples' lack of understanding as to what their assignment was to be? About his return? About his departure? About concern for others? About his mission? About his divinity?

12. In the light of their background and their notions about Jesus as Christ, what were some clarifications and extensions they would be needing in order to sense what the ministering of the Holy Spirit was going to be?
13. How would the apostles have difficulty in sensing how they might experience the divine presence when the physical Jesus would not be with them? What spiritual radiance went out from Jesus' person that they might expect in the Holy Spirit?
14. E. Stanley Jones is credited with the statement that the early Christians did not say in dismay, "Look what the world has come to!" but that they said in hope and joy, "Look who has come into the world!" And what about modern saints?
15. How was the conference in Jerusalem, described in Acts I, an essential in the experience of those disciples in getting ready for endowment? What happened in this conference that indicated they were on the way?
16. How was what the Holy Spirit was to be doing a continuing of what Jesus had been doing with his apostles and other disciples?

CONSIDERATION ELEVEN

1. What do you see Jesus doing before his departure to prepare his men for the Day of Pentecost?
2. What do you think the twelve apostles expected would happen when "the empowerment" would come to them?
3. How was the Day of Pentecost a contributive setting for this happening?

4. What did the disciples do after the departure of Jesus to make themselves ready for this endowing by the Holy Spirit?

5. How were the happenings of "the wind" and "the fire" in accord with Jewish notions about the expressions of God? Note their idea of the *ruah* as "the breath of God" that was breathed into man. Note their cherished story of Moses as "the burning bush." Do you see these first happenings at Pentecost as "attention-getters," as symbolic expressions, as foundational? What is lost when these are held up as the major happenings of Pentecost?

6. How is it important that we see that in glossolalia these disciples said something that had content?

7. A basic criticism of "tongue-talking" today is that it has chiefly momentary exhilaration without message, without relation to "the business of living." How did the Pentecost glossolalia rise above this?

8. When Peter held out to his hearers the promise of the coming of the Holy Spirit, what counsel do you consider these hearers needed about the ministry of the Holy Spirit? What do you think they expected?

9. What instruction, what experience would these "baptized believers" need concerning the continuing ministry of the Holy Spirit?

10. How might glossolalia and other dramatic happenings be used as publicity headlines? How did this function as more than this?

11. What does the picture of the Jerusalem congregation of disciples (Acts 2:41-47) disclose about their living together in Christian fellowship? How does this give a picture of wholesome spirituality?

12. What is your reaction to the view that Pentecost was "the birthday of the church"? How do you see that Jesus brought his church into being? Or do you see this as the continuing and the confirming of the church?

13. How does the picture of the disciples in Jerusalem after Pentecost confirm the conception that the Church of Jesus Christ is "a fellowship of Saints on mission"? What was the functioning of the Holy Spirit in this fellowship?

14. What significance was there for the early Christians when they discovered that they could experience the "divine presence" without the bodily presence of Jesus?

15. How was the ministering of the Spirit on Pentecost Day a universalizing ministry?

16. Apply the following comment to contemporary groups that emphasize "tongues" and "the Spirit": "A movement is measured by what is left out as well as by what is included." Apply to our own contemporary church.

17. How do the songs of a group indicate their notions about the Holy Spirit? What messages are we needing in hymns today that express adequately our beliefs and our experiences about the Holy Spirit then and now?

18. What do you see should happen in a contemporary Day of Pentecost through the ministry of the Holy Spirit? What "universalizing" should follow?

CONSIDERATION TWELVE

1. How would Paul's own experience in conversion and calling enter into his instruction about the Holy Spirit? What did he see had happened in him?

2. How did Paul and Peter make the experiencing of the Holy Spirit coming to the Gentiles the foundation of their position for taking the gospel to Gentiles over against the position of the legalistic Jewish Christians in the conference of Jerusalem, c. A.D. 49 (Acts 15)? What

247

did these men say had happened that evidenced that Gentiles should be received as Christians without having to comply with Jewish legalistic requirements?

3. How did Paul minister to "converts" in Ephesus concerning the Holy Spirit? What would he need to explain to them about this Spirit?

4. Paul wrote about "fruits of the Spirit" and about "gifts of the Spirit." Functionally how are these two aspects of the ministry of the Holy Spirit to be distinguished? How may they be viewed as two functioning aspects of the inclusive field of the ministry of the Holy Spirit?

5. What did Paul mean by *edification* when he set this forth as the requirement for wholesome ministry of the Spirit? When would you consider that a contemporary congregation or reunion or camp would be "edified"?

6. Why did "tongues" have so strong an appeal to many early Christians? How did Paul evaluate the "gift of tongues"? How did the experience of *tongues* in Corinth differ in purpose and in influence from glossolalia on the Day of Pentecost?

7. What is the basic meaning of *charisma?* How did Paul use this word? In Paul's use of the word what would mark a truly *charismatic* person?

8. Interpret and consider this observation: "When the grace of God is thought of as the power of God, the Holy Spirit tends to lose rightful place and meaning."

9. How does Paul relate the *grace of God* and the *Spirit of God?* How are the two to be complementary, but not identical?

10. Contrast the intent and the desire to "know" that Jesus is Christ by a single, one-time miraculous experience with intent to "know" through continuing experience with Christ through the knowing through the ministry of the Holy Spirit.

11. Evaluate and interpret and apply this comment, "I

would have to live a long while with Christ Jesus in order to 'catch on' that he is divine, that he is Christ." What understanding of Christ through living with him is required in order to "know" him? How do we get to know persons?

12. How did Paul see his living with the Holy Spirit as continuing his meeting with Jesus Christ on the Damascus way?

13. One translation of the story of Paul's contact with Jesus Christ on the Damascus way has Jesus asking, "Saul, is it hard for you to fight against yourself?" What inner struggles and tensions were going on in Saul? How were these resolved and inner harmony achieved as Saul got with Christ through his Spirit?

14. Interpret and apply "the gift of discernment" in the light of Paul's inclusive approach to the ministering of the Holy Spirit. What qualities in a person would qualify this person for this gift? What studies would help the person to qualify? What would be the purpose for the exercising of this gift?

15. In Paul's dissertation on agape in Chapter 13 of the First Letter to the Corinthian congregation, what does he set forth as distinguishing qualities of this love? Contrast this with some contemporary notions about love.

16. What qualities, taken together, did Paul see would be working together in the person who has met Jesus and has received the Holy Spirit? What would constitute a new creation? (See II Cor. 5:17 ff.)

17. How would a congregation, a church need to understand and appreciate the Holy Spirit in Paul's day in order to experience this Spirit in achieving evangelizing, harmonizing, revealing experience for a branch of the church with spiritual vitality and spiritual vision? Without this Spirit what other measures might be used to get oneness and increase? What kind of increase?

1. How did the view that in former times scriptural writings were written under the impulsion of the Holy Spirit give a certain finality that would release from the need for the continuing ministry of the Holy Spirit?
2. After the church organization and the canon of scripture were definitized, who had the authority to interpret scripture?
3. How may a movement such as Montanism declare the need for spiritual renewal yet set forth a conception of spiritual vitality and endowment that can get in the way of wholesome spiritual revival? How may emphasis on what is wrong get in the way of bringing to pass what is right?
4. How may a movement set forth such a limited notion of what constitutes revelation through the Holy Spirit that it blocks the way to genuine enlightenment? What can happen when a small group such as the inner group of the Gnostics take the view that they are the ones through whom God is enlightening, and only they?
5. What situations impelled Christians to select a fixed canon and to formulate a fixed creed? What happens when such a finalization becomes definitely fixed?
6. How do you explain the small attention given to the Holy Spirit during those creed-forming days? Do these factors apply today?
7. How did the institutionalized church interpret the functioning of grace? How would the church administer this grace?
8. How does the controversy over the "filioque" clause illustrate how a church can be divided by arguments about things that are supposed to unite? How much

concern was there about the Holy Spirit in this long conflict? What were the real issues?

9. What do you consider a healthy formulating of creeds and a healthy using of creeds? How might a statement of dogma about the Holy Spirit get in the way of future exploration and revelation? How can fixed words block useful meaning?

10. Contrast and illustrate organization as means or as master. What factors made Christians of the fourth century and after so interested in the organization and administration of the church?

11. What is your reaction to the comment that religion needs no organization, that the Holy Spirit is to guide and unite? Consider the church as a living organism. How is organization essential to living?

12. How do you go to Paul's writings in an inclusive way when someone says to you that we are "saved by grace"? That we are "not saved by works"?

13. How is the ministry of the Holy Spirit endangered by assuming that this Spirit is supernatural and is not to be considered? What constitutes a wholesome viewing of and considering of the Holy Spirit?

14. Could the church of the fourth century and after have developed a functioning organization and experienced the continuing ministry of the Holy Spirit? What guidelines do you set forth for such functioning?

15. What would be your reaction to having members of the plenary session of our general conference stand up and say together, "We believe in the Holy Spirit"?

1. How would Martin Luther's own sense of sinfulness condition what he would emphasize as important in his statement of beliefs and means to salvation? What was his conception of the nature of man and the needs of man?

2. How did Martin Luther make the Bible the new authority to replace the old authority of the priesthood-led and sacrament-operated Roman Catholic Church? How did he evaluate the Scriptures in order that he might have adequate authority for his reformation? How did he consider the Scriptures came to be?

3. How did Martin Luther make salvation a happening in which man is only the recipient? How did he see faith and grace having such a basic part in this deliverance of man from damnation? From what did Martin Luther see man being saved?

4. What was the effect on the German Reformation of the translating of the Scriptures into the German language while Luther was in Wartburg Castle? How did he tie the Holy Scriptures to the Holy Spirit?

5. It is said that creeds and confessions list beliefs on the things that are issues at the time of the formation of these documents. How does this explain in part why the Lutheran documents say so little about the Holy Spirit, yet presume the Spirit? What were the main theological concerns in Luther's day?

6. What kind of God did John Calvin pray and preach? What quality of Holy Spirit would attend such a God as Calvin's? How is a person's conception of the Holy Spirit conditioned by this person's conception of God?

7. In Calvinist theology would a person know whether or not he was elected? Here *election* means designated by

God for salvation. Was the "elected" person to have any experience of the Holy Spirit?

8. What were the main concerns of those who managed the breakaway from the Roman Catholic Church in England? What were the major topics emphasized in the Thirty-nine Articles? What was said about the Holy Spirit? Why was so little said?

9. Interpret and evaluate this comment: "The Reformers legalized the Spirit, but they never vitalized the Church with this Spirit." To what extent and how do you ascribe or not ascribe to this statement?

10. Why and how were the several leaders of the Protestant Reformation so concerned with developing creeds and confessions? Could they have survived without these? When and how is a creed beneficial? When not beneficial?

11. What is to be a wholesome belief about the functioning of the Holy Spirit in the producing and the using of a creed?

12. What did Quakers mean by "inner light"? Do you see them meaning ministry of the Holy Spirit? What was to happen in a person when he experienced this "inner light"? How did this belief call forth so much opposition? Would you characterize the experience of the Holy Spirit as "inner light"?

13. Reconstruct the setting out of which Luther wrote the hymn, "A Mighty Fortress" about 1529. What was Luther saying to himself and his people? What do you see him saying in "The Spirit and the gifts are ours"? How did he see the Spirit functioning in the life of the person?

14. Evaluate and apply this comment of Henry Van Dusen in *Spirit, Son and Father:* "It is becoming increasingly recognized, at long last, that classic Protestantism was far from the thoroughgoing revolution which tradition has pictured, and that its reclamation of original

253

Christianity was far from radical and complete" (pp. 80, 81). Apply this to the Holy Spirit.

15. Apply in a constructive way the observation that the Holy Spirit needs to be emancipated from "the dead-hand of tradition" and from "the leading-strings of dogma" (H. P. Van Dusen), that this Spirit may bring fresh guidance and vitality. Apply to the Reformation period. Apply today.

16. What points of guidance can come to us out of some far-out movements that focus on "the Spirit" with emphasis on exuberance without examination? What kinds of things can happen?

17. What do you see as foremost contributions to the religious life of the world that came out of "the Reformation"? What else would you like to have had happen in this Reformation? Do you see God going as far as he could then under the circumstances?

CONSIDERATION FIFTEEN

1. What is your reaction to the comment that God took a recess from human affairs on earth during the Dark Ages?

2. What was happening in the world of man during the millennium from c. 600 to 1600 that, when pieced together, would indicate that God was not on recess? What happenings, what developments were laying foundations for future spiritual happenings?

3. How long and how much did God make ready for the opening of the Western world so there could be some

spiritual revivalistic and restoration happenings in religion?

4. How did some believers who came to the West for religious freedom tend to turn about and lay down requirements in religion for others to meet? How is a group who consider themselves as having the "full truth" tempted to set down stipulations for others? Give examples of what happened in colonial days in America. Why did this not work here?

5. What factors combined to make the time of the Revolutionary period and after a time of low spirituality in the new nation? Note the word *factors*. This word suggests an approach different from the approach that uses the word *fault*. We inquire about *factors* rather than about *faults*.

6. It is said that the Great Awakening and the Second Awakening stressed the themes of "hell fire and damnation." What place would there be for the Holy Spirit in the thinking of the revivalists?

7. During the Great Revival period what bodily expressions came to be considered manifestations of the Holy Spirit? Why were these manifestations wanted? How did some not seeking these bodily manifestations get involved in them? What body manifestations do you consider rightly associated with the Spirit?

8. There are three common explanations of overt manifestations: (1) They are of God; (2) they are of the devil; (3) they are of human generation. What explanation do you prefer? How and why is blaming the devil an "easy way out"?

9. How did "the manifestations of the Spirit" produce differences between and conflicts between church groups? Note the comment, "The pseudo spirit divides; the genuine Spirit unites."

10. Some critics said that during some revival camp meetings "babies got conceived, but not by the Holy Ghost." How may a love-everybody atmosphere with dismissal of restraints in conduct bring on undesirable social relations?

11. An adverse criticism of revival camps was that the life of the camp was usually supervised and that the preaching was unrelated to the business of good living. How might the doctrine of "faith without works" enter here? How do you respond to the comment, "The Holy Ghost prompts to loving and not to living"?

12. How were the revivals indicating some spiritual hungers that were in the people of these times and places? In what ways were the churches of those times not meeting the needs and the hungers of the people? What hungers in our members and in others should we recognize and endeavor to meet today? How shall we evaluate what persons are wanting?

13. What might have been the reaction of these revivalists to those who might have held forth a wholesome message and wholesome experience of the Holy Spirit?

14. What kind of preaching was considered Spirit-led in those camp meetings? What are some notions about what constitutes Spirit-led preaching in our times? What do you consider worthy criteria of Spirit-led preaching?

15. How might revival happenings be used to lay foundation and motivation for wholesome incitation toward and wholesome experience of the Holy Spirit? How would you lead on from such revivalism?

cheville, Roy A.

AUTHOR

Spiritual Resources

TITLE

are available Today Volume1

DATE DUE	BORROWER'S NAME